New Directions
for Social Work
Practice Research

New Directions for Social Work Practice Research

Miriam Potocky-Tripodi and
Tony Tripodi, *Editors*

NASW PRESS

National Association of Social Workers
Washington, DC

Josephine A. V. Allen, PhD, ACSW, *President*
Josephine Nieves, MSW, PhD, *Executive Director*

Paula L. Delo, *Executive Editor*

Steph Selice, *Senior Editor*

William Schroeder, *Staff Editor*

Sharon Lamberton, Editorial Solutions, *Copy Editor*

Nedalina Dineva, Editorial Services, Inc., *Indexer*

Chanté Lampton, *Acquisitions Associate*

Heather Peters, *Editorial Secretary*

Cover by The Watermark Design Office, Alexandria, VA

Typeset, printed, and bound by Mack Printing Group, Ephrata, PA

© 1999 by the NASW Press

Library of Congress Cataloging-in-Publication Data

New directions for social work practice research / editors, Miriam
   Potocky-Tripodi and Tony Tripodi.
     p.   cm.
   Includes bibliographical references and index.
   ISBN 0-87101-305-3 (alk. paper)
   1. Social service—Research.   2. Human services—Research.
3. Evaluation research (Social action programs)   I. Potocky
-Tripodi, Miriam.   II. Tripodi, Tony.
HV11.N486   1999
361.3'2'072—DC21   99-12763
                                                              CIP

Printed in the United States of America

To the memory of Scott Briar,
a pioneer of new directions in practice research

Contents

Introduction

Miriam Potocky-Tripodi and Tony Tripodi

Two seminal articles in the early 1970s—"Is casework effective?" (Fischer, 1973), and "The age of accountability" (Briar, 1973)—began 25 years of scholarship in social work research that has generated a large body of literature on practice research. Milestones have included the explication and promotion of the single-system design (for example, Bloom, Fischer, & Orme, 1995; Tripodi, 1994) and measurement methods for clinical practice (for example, Blythe & Tripodi, 1989; Fischer & Corcoran, 1994). Together these approaches to practice research have come to be known as the empirical clinical practice movement or the scientist-practitioner model. Another advancement has been the articulation of a research approach for intervention design and development (for example, Rothman & Thomas, 1994). Critiques of the scientist-practitioner model have used pragmatic (for example, Bronson, 1994), ethical (for example, Gibbs, 1994), epistemological (for example, Heineman, 1981; Tyson, 1992), and political (for example, Davis, 1994) arguments.

Several organizational initiatives also were undertaken during this period to promote research, including practice research, in social work. The 1984 Council on Social Work Education accreditation standards mandated the inclusion of content on practice evaluation in the social work curriculum. The National Institute of Mental Health Task Force on Social Work Research, established in 1988, examined the research resources in social work and recommended ways to strengthen those resources. And the Institute for the Advancement of Social Work Research and the Society for Social Work and Research were founded in 1994 for the purpose of supporting and promoting research in the profession.

Periodically, scholars in the field have produced thoughtful reflections on these developments. Three notable examples are Videka-Sherman and Reid's 1990 book, *Advances in Clinical Social Work Research*; Grasso and Epstein's 1992 book, *Research Utilization in the Social Services*; and a special issue of *Social Work Research* (June 1996) in which a panel of

1

scholars reviewed and reacted to three recent books on the scientist-practitioner approach.

Videka-Sherman and Reid's edited volume was the product of a 1988 conference on empiricism in clinical practice. Many contributors reflected on the present status and future prospects of social work research in four specific areas: single-system designs (SSDs), methodological advances, research utilization, and epistemology.

The editors drew several conclusions. They noted an evolution in single-system designs from "a fervent, unqualified commitment to the strict use of SSDs by all clinical social workers" to "a more thoughtful, tempered approach that is based on the experience of a decade" (p. 419). This more tempered approach advocates the use of single-system designs for assessment, goal setting, and monitoring rather than for establishing causal connections between interventions and outcomes. It is recognized by most social work researchers that the latter purpose is best achieved through controlled group designs. Videka-Sherman and Reid also noted "increased . . . concern about the growing schism between clinical researchers and clinical practitioners" (p. 419). In view of evidence indicating that practitioners rarely utilize research findings, the editors expressed the need for the development of research approaches that are relevant to practitioners. Videka-Sherman and Reid also predicted that computer technology would have a profound impact on practice research in the future. Finally, they noted increasing methodological diversity among social work researchers, as exemplified by increased attention to qualitative methodologies, process as well as outcome studies, and issues of clinical significance.

Grasso and Epstein's book also was an edited volume based on a conference, this one on research utilization. Five themes were addressed: (1) changing models of practice in research utilization; (2) research utilization in interpersonal practice; (3) research utilization in administration and community organization; (4) putting research to work in agency settings; and (5) educating for research utilization. A major implication that arose was "the need to reconcile utilization issues with organizational issues, with larger system issues, and with direct service delivery issues" (p. 448). Grasso and Epstein also hailed the personal computer as a means of making such research utilization and integration possible. Finally, while recognizing that education for research utilization is primarily the function of schools of social work, they saw opportunities for the development of new educational models through agency-university collaborations.

The book forum that constituted the June 1996 issue of *Social Work Research* was stimulated by three books: Bloom, Fischer, and Orme's (1995) *Evaluating Practice*; Blythe, Tripodi, and Briar's (1994) *Direct Practice Research in Human Service Agencies*; and Fischer and Corcoran's (1994) *Measures for Clinical Practice*. Journal Editor Stuart Kirk selected the books to serve as a point of departure for reflection on the status and impact of the scientist-practitioner model. The eight panelists who responded expressed a wide variety of views. Witkin argued that the assumptions and constraints of empirical clinical practice methodologies "favor certain forms of understanding over others" (p. 73). He suggested social constructionism as an alternative approach for demonstrating accountability. In contrast, Thyer lauded the accomplishments of the empirical clinical practice movement and advocated for its extension through the adoption of professional ethical standards that would address clients' rights to empirically supported effective treatments. Wakefield and Kirk argued that "the methods of the scientist-practitioner model are of unproved clinical effectiveness, limited scientific value, questionable practicality, and unknown net benefits" (p. 83). However, they also argued against postmodernist approaches (such as the social constructionism advocated by Witkin). Wakefield and Kirk declared it "critical that we use scientific research methods to study practice and to try to make it more effective" (p. 93), but they also expressed the belief that such endeavors belong in the domain of the researcher, not in the domain of the practitioner.

Irwin Epstein asserted that "the research-based strategies and requirements of single-subject studies directly conflict with the professional culture and values of social work" (p. 99). In marked contradiction to Thyer's position on ethical standards, Epstein claimed that "practice-research strategies probably violate the NASW Code of Ethics" (p. 99). He then described recent developments in practice evaluation that he viewed as positive. These included growing recognition of the potential contributions of qualitative research and practice wisdom, and emphasis on consumer satisfaction. Meyer argued that "the emphasis on scientific practice . . . is a unique feature of behavioral practice-research" (p. 104), and that the reductionism inherent in this approach is antithetical to the complex systems in which clients live and practice takes place. She stressed "a need for research emphasis on developing substantive knowledge to better understand what practice is about" (p. 101).

While expressing support for the scientist-practitioner model, Rosen noted the failure of most practitioners to incorporate it into their practice. He described several elements of the model that he believed hindered its acceptance and application. Finally, Laura Epstein criticized both current research and practice as being grounded in psychic determinism, focusing on intrapsychic rather than environmental influences on personal problems. Like Meyer, she viewed the practitioner-researcher model as inappropriate given the complex systems that constitute social reality.

This book has been created in the same spirit of reflective analysis as the Videka-Sherman and Reid, the Grasso and Epstein, and the *Social Work Research* compilations. Its purpose is to provide a critical assessment of the current status of social work practice research and to identify new directions for the future. Such reflection is timely as the social work profession enters its second century and the new millennium.

Like the Videka-Sherman and Reid and the Grasso and Epstein books, the current volume is a product of a conference on practice research. As such, it also extends the themes in those books from the perspective of a decade later. The conference, titled "Research for Social Work Practice," was held in January 1998 at Florida International University in North Miami, Florida. In addition to Florida International University, conference co-sponsors were the Society for Social Work and Research, the Institute for the Advancement of Social Work Research, and the University of Huddersfield, England. This meeting was a follow-up to inaugural conferences on social work research held by those organizations in 1995 ("Advancing Knowledge for Human Services," a national conference held in Washington, DC, in April; and "Evaluation of Social Work Practice," an international conference held at Huddersfield in September). One of the intents of the conference sponsors was to lay a foundation for future annual social work research conferences in the United States, and periodic conferences at Huddersfield (which would attract more European participants).

The chapters in this book comprise five invitational papers that were presented at the Florida conference. The invited speakers were all leading scholars of social work practice research from the United States and United Kingdom. Each speaker was asked to prepare a presentation on a specific topic related to the broad conference theme of research for social work practice. Consequently, the five chapters together provide a mixture of historical, conceptual, empirical, and pragmatic perspectives on the theme.

To set the context for the consideration of new directions for social work practice research, the book begins with a historical account and analysis of social work research over the past 100 years by Alfred J. Kahn. In his keynote address to the 1998 conference, Kahn (1998) noted that

> at the beginning, social work shared its heritage with social science; the two grew apart but never fully separated as social work explored and built up its expertise in what we now call practice. Then, in a series of "bursts," the research of the profession concentrated on the social survey, on statistics and social indicators, on what we would now call "policy"—all before the 1950s call for evaluative research. The 1948 founding of a specialized research association, the Social Work Research Group (SWRG) coincided with the evaluation movement and SWRG—along with other specialized associations—was absorbed into the National Association of Social Workers during one of the profession's generic thrusts. All of the earlier research tendencies continued while new emphases appeared. By the 1970s, social work research had become as broad and diverse as the profession, as social work developed in many new subfields of practice, even as it concentrated on its "micro" practice and increasingly gave up much of the "macro." Despite the enormous quantitative expansion, scholars of the field complain of the failure of research to meet the field's need for knowledge and of the unrelatedness of research and practice. Social work research at its most sophisticated is now conducted from a social-behavioral science base, even while experts in those fields increasingly are involved in what the profession might define as its research and practice. (p. 1)

One of the important implications of Kahn's historical analysis is that the future of social work practice research has roots in the past. Indeed, the influence of social science continues to be present, especially in methodology. Furthermore, many of the debates on social work practice research, such as those addressed in the book forum described above, have already been played out in the social sciences.

In Chapter 2, Aaron Rosen, Enola K. Proctor, and Marlys M. Staudt examine the readiness of the social work profession to establish guidelines for effective practice. The chapter addresses the question, "Is social work research capable of guiding practice?" Proctor, Rosen, and Staudt conducted a content analysis of all articles published in 13 major social work journals from 1993 to 1997. They found that about half of these articles reported on empirical studies. These articles were then categorized according to the type of knowledge they generated: descriptive, explanatory, or control, with the latter being intervention effectiveness studies (in other words, studies that are capable of yielding practice guidelines). The authors found that only 7 percent of all articles fell into this latter category. Further analysis examined the specificities of the interventions and outcomes described in the articles. The authors conclude that the development of guidelines for social work practice is hampered by a paucity of control studies in which interventions and outcomes are adequately specified.

We support Proctor, Rosen, and Staudt's call for more control studies; however, we also do not wish to devalue the contributions of descriptive and explanatory studies. Elsewhere, Tripodi (1985) has identified levels of knowledge similar to the typology offered by Proctor, Rosen, and Staudt, and noted that each higher level needs to build on the lower ones. Thus, descriptive and explanatory studies should feed into the development of control studies. The problem, in our view, is that this rarely occurs. Few social work researchers pursue a focused and sustained research agenda that progressively builds knowledge in a particular problem area and ultimately results in the development and testing of interventions for that problem. There are probably many reasons for this, some of which are mentioned by Proctor, Rosen, and Staudt. We believe that such obstacles need to be overcome, and we urge more developmental intervention research of the type articulated by Rothman and Thomas (1994).

In Chapter 3, Mansoor A. F. Kazi "reviews the main contemporary trends in practice research in England. The review is based on some of the key publications on evaluation of social work practice that have emerged between 1995 and 1997 and on the recent experience of the Centre for Evaluation Studies at the University of Huddersfield. The chapter begins with the complexities of effectiveness in social work, then proceeds to critically analyze the contributions and limitations of each of the main research paradigms in apprehending the realities of social work practice and its effectiveness. These perspectives are identified as empirical practice, pragmatism, critical theory, and scientific realism—the latter being a new addition" (p. 56). Kazi states that "[scientific realism] brings together almost all of the other main perspectives, attempts a white box evaluation of practice, addressing the effects, the inner workings and operations of the components of the program, and how they are connected. It attempts to reveal not only what works in social work practice, but also what works for whom, and in what contexts" (p. 76).

We support Kazi's moderate stance on these epistemological issues. In contrast to the polarization that seems to characterize much of the U.S. literature on the topic, Kazi recognizes and insightfully articulates both the advantages and disadvantages of each paradigm. We, too, favor the scientific realism approach, which entails, in part, selecting appropriate methodologies based on the nature of the research question. While much of our own individual research and scholarship has been within the "positivistic" paradigm (or, as Kazi points out, positivistic paradigms), we believe that alternate approaches—particularly those that have been combined under the rubric of "qualitative" approaches—are entirely appropriate for certain research questions.

In Chapter 4, Roger Fuller describes the Practitioner Research Programme at the Social Work Research Centre at the University of Stirling, Scotland. The chapter begins with an examination of the historically uneasy relationship between social work practice and research, and briefly reviews some of the political factors that have influenced this relationship. The chapter then describes the aforementioned program, whose aim is to bridge the practice-research gap. During the nine-month training program, participants are provided support in conducting research projects within their agencies. The chapter describes the program structure, the participants, their research questions, their methodologies, and their support needs. Fuller concludes with an assessment of the strengths and limitations of this training approach, and suggests a new direction for the future of practice research: a model of "reflexive practice . . . a practice that is capable of learning from experience and adapting itself to the lessons learned" (p. 90).

To our knowledge, the practitioner research program has no direct parallel in the United States, although there are several examples of agency-based research. Thus, this training program can serve as a model for adaptation and adoption in this country. One of the recurring themes throughout this volume is the practitioner-researcher gap that seems to persist despite efforts to bridge it. The Practitioner Research Programme at the University of Stirling provides a method for making research relevant to practitioners and engaging them in it, in a different way from the scientist-practitioner model. The "research-minded practice" model proposed by Fuller goes beyond the use of single-system designs, incorporating a broad range of methodologies (p. 82). Also, as Fuller notes, it moves away from "straight" evaluation, into a more critical stance addressing the context of practice (pp. 81–82).

In Chapter 5, David M. Austin examines research resource developments in the United States against the background of the 1991 report of the National Institute of Mental Health Task Force on Social Work Research. The chapter "focuses on nationally visible research developments intended to contribute to the general body of knowledge used by social work practitioners and by other human service specialists" (p. 92). The chapter examines the following topics: research development centers, national social work research support infrastructures; research training; research curriculum development; technical assistance; research dissemination; social work research domains; doctoral education; and research funding support. The chapter concludes by identifying areas of action that still need to be addressed.

Among the important points raised by Austin is the absence of a concerted effort to develop social work research resources in substantive areas other than mental health. Clearly, the scope of social work extends beyond this one field of practice, and research should be supported accordingly. In a similar vein, we would add that research on macro practice should have equal footing with clinical research. Another critical point, made by Austin and also addressed by Kahn, pertains to the "convenience factor" in social work research. Researchers often study topics and populations that are convenient for them rather than concentrate on building a focused research agenda that, over a career lifetime, would generate some cumulative body of knowledge on a particular practice issue.

We return to these points in the conclusion, synthesize the material presented in each of the chapters, and provide a summary action agenda for the future of social work practice research.

References

Bloom, M., Fischer, J., & Orme, J. G. (1995). *Evaluating practice: Guidelines for the accountable professional* (2nd ed). Needham Heights, MA: Allyn & Bacon.

Blythe, B. J., & Tripodi, T. (1989). *Measurement in direct practice.* Newbury Park, CA: Sage.

Blythe, B. J., Tripodi, T., & Briar, S. (1994). *Direct practice research in human service agencies.* New York: Columbia University Press.

Briar, S. (1973). The age of accountability. *Social Work, 18,* 2.

Bronson, D. E. (1994). Is a scientist-practitioner model appropriate for direct social work practice? No. In W. W. Hudson & P. S. Nurius (Eds.), *Controversial issues in social work research* (pp. 81–86). Boston: Allyn & Bacon.

Davis, L. V. (1994). Is feminist research inherently qualitative, and is it a fundamentally different approach to research? Yes. In W. W. Hudson & P. S. Nurius (Eds.), *Controversial issues in social work research* (pp. 63–68). Boston: Allyn & Bacon.

Epstein, I. (1996). In quest of a research-based model for clinical practice: Or, why can't a social worker be more like a researcher? *Social Work Research, 20,* 97–100.

Epstein, L. (1996). The trouble with the researcher-practitioner idea. *Social Work Research, 20,* 113–117.

Fischer, J. (1973). Is casework effective? A review. *Social Work, 18,* 107–110.

Fischer, J., & Corcoran, K. (1994). *Measures for clinical practice: A sourcebook* (2nd ed.). New York: Free Press.

Gibbs, L. E. (1994). Is a scientist-practitioner model appropriate for social work administrative practice? No. In W. W. Hudson & P. S. Nurius (Eds.), *Controversial issues in social work research* (pp. 135–140). Boston: Allyn & Bacon.

Grasso, A. J., & Epstein, I. (Eds.) (1992). *Research utilization in the social services: Innovations for practice and administration.* Binghamton, NY: Haworth Press.

Heineman, M. B. (1981). The obsolete scientific imperative in social work research. *Social Service Review,* 55, 371–397.

Kahn, A. J. (1998). *The social work research domain in historical perspective: The first hundred years.* Paper presented at the annual meeting of the Society for Social Work and Research, North Miami, FL.

Meyer, C. H. (1996). My son the scientist. *Social Work Research, 20,* 101–104.

Rosen, A. (1996). The scientific practitioner revisited: Some obstacles and prerequisites for fuller implementation in practice. *Social Work Research, 20,* 105–111.

Rothman, J., & Thomas, E. J. (Eds.) (1994). *Intervention research: Design and development for human service.* Binghamton, NY: Haworth Press.

Thyer, B. A. (1996). Forty years of progress toward empirical clinical practice? *Social Work Research, 20,* 77–81.

Tripodi, T. (1985). Research designs. In R. M. Grinnell, Jr. (Ed.), *Social Work Research and Evaluation* (2nd ed.; pp. 231–259). Itasca, IL: F. E. Peacock Publishers.

Tripodi, T. (1994). *A primer on single-subject design for clinical social workers.* Washington, DC: NASW Press.

Tyson, K. B. (1992). A new approach to relevant scientific research for practitioners: The heuristic paradigm. *Social Work, 37,* 541–556.

Videka-Sherman, L., & Reid, W. J. (Eds.) (1990). *Advances in clinical social work research.* Washington, DC: NASW Press.

Wakefield, J. C., & Kirk, S. A. (1996). Unscientific thinking about scientific practice: Evaluating the scientist-practitioner model. *Social Work Research, 20,* 83–95.

Witkin, S. L. (1996). If empirical practice is the answer, what is the question? *Social Work Research, 20,* 69–75.

CHAPTER 1

The Social Work Research Domain in Historical Perspective: The First 100 Years

Alfred J. Kahn

Zimbalist (1977) concluded our only available extensive history of social work research with a concept of its scope. He defined it as research on a problem or question arising in the practice or the planning of social welfare services or social work programs (undifferentiated until recent years); research under the auspices of (or funded by) a social work agency; and research published in a social work journal or disseminated through other social work channels. Zimbalist's definition is not tight but rather realistic, if perhaps incomplete. He saw the development of the field as occurring around distinct, if overlapping, "waves" or "cycles" of emphasis, each coherent and self-contained and each, in turn, the research preoccupation of its period.[1] While a few of his "cycles" do fit the formula, I have concluded that the overall scheme does not quite hold up, since several "cycles" have vague beginning dates but do not quite end. Indeed, I shall argue, social work research is constantly broadening its scope, and some of the preoccupations repeat from time to time.

At the Beginning: The Shared Heritage of Social Work and Social Science

Two streams of social action converged to launch the social work profession a century ago, an event marked by the first educational offerings by what is now the Columbia University School of Social Work. One stream comprised the friendly visitors of the Charity Organization Societies (COSs) and Associations for the Improvement of the Conditions of the Poor (AICPs), the children's aid societies, residential institutions, and other charitable institutions whose volunteers were increasingly supplemented by paid agents and administrators. Poor Law officials and employees of the expanding state welfare boards also were part of this group. The other stream comprised the new scholars of the urban industrial society who, after the Civil War, began to free themselves from the moralistic and deductive thinking patterns of 18th- and early 19th-century scholarship. When most university classical programs featured education, moral science, and religion, these new scholars turned to history, political economy, history of reform, and psychological development in the hope of understanding the problems of their day and contributing to solutions.

The first national social science grouping, the American Social Science Association (ASSA), convened in 1865 not as a learned society in the modern sense, but as a forum for exchange of objective information about problems, reform movements, history, and administration. The group created sections on education, health, finance, and jurisprudence. In 1873 the group added a section on social economy in the conviction, according to Bruno (1948, 1957), that the application of science to problems in human relationships would result in discovery and improvements. The purpose of modern social science as it was being shaped was "to promote human welfare" (Bruno, 1957, p. 5).

By 1876, with Johns Hopkins as the major center of innovation, a new university model began to evolve. At the center of this model were professors who carried out investigations, used their research as a basis for teaching, and disseminated findings through publication. Early graduate students both learned and contributed to this process through field investigations in support of the professors' research. Their foci were poverty, tenement house conditions, tuberculosis, almshouses, and more. In her extraordinary unpublished dissertation, Betty Broadhurst (1971) traces the paths taken from Hopkins (the "mother house") to Wisconsin, Chicago, Stanford, Harvard, Columbia, and another dozen colleges and universities as Hopkins graduates founded or joined modern social science departments. At the same time, social welfare programs were moving toward the systematization and rational planning then called *scientific*.

Many leading programs recruited young scholars into administrative and executive posts, giving the emerging social work profession a cadre of research-experienced and social science-educated professionals who were to make a major mark on social welfare programs in the late 19th and early 20th centuries.

The Hopkins-trained scholars and their counterparts from other academic centers continued for some decades in what became three streams of work: (1) the effort to develop basic theory in sociology and other evolving behavioral and social sciences; (2) applied investigation with a reform objective; and (3) the undertaking to train people to do the practical work in what was to be social work. In a story painstakingly assembled by Broadhurst (but too detailed to fully recount here)[2] one group of these new-type scholars (including Philip Ayres) joined an effort pushed at the practical end by people like Ann L. Dawes, Mary Richmond, Zilpha Smith, and others, to launch formal education in *applied philanthropy*. Some of the lecturers in the early programs were the same social scientists who were founding the new social science departments in many places. Other lecturers were program leaders and practice pioneers. And the early schools (Broadhurst, 1971; Meier, 1954) struggled for some time with the balance between the academic lectures (which came from the social science tradition) and practical work (agency visits, observation and, finally, fieldwork). Lectures and theory courses from the how-to-do-it side would develop slowly.

The streams eventually diverged, although some ties remained for a long time: in many social work schools the social scientists continue to teach the research courses. By 1874, state board directors spun off from the mainstream of the ASSA to create a section on Social Economy which soon became known as the National Conference on Charities and Corrections (and later, the National Conference of Social Welfare). Other spin-offs had established the National (American) Prison Association (1870) and the American Public Health Association (1872). Moving in the other direction were those scholars who created the American Historical Association (1884). The ASSA had outlived its mixed purposes.

My point is this: In the empiricism and pragmatism of the post–Civil War period, particularly as 1890 approached, social research was a shared activity. The academic side of the newly consolidated social work profession and the exploding new social sciences developed from the different tendencies in one body. Amos Warner's *American Charities* (1894), the first social work text, was written by a Johns Hopkins Ph.D. who wrote his dissertation while serving as general secretary of the Baltimore Charity Organization Society (COS). His chapters rely heavily on the new research. Mary Richmond wrote the second required text[3] in 1898, *Friendly Visiting Among the Poor*. Richmond followed Warner as general secretary in Baltimore and later had a similar role in Philadelphia before moving on to head the Charity Organization Department of the newly established Russell Sage Foundation in 1909. She was interested in and drew on empirical data and recognized that environmental issues required attention if COS clients were to be helped, although she adopted a medical metaphor for her practice formulations. It should be recalled, moreover, that her later major work, *Social Diagnosis* (1917) was a report on prevailing practice based on systematic data collection from various fields of practice. In some of the curriculum debates during the first decade of the New York School, Richmond advocated more from the practice than from the academic side because she considered the offerings unbalanced; however, neither she nor her practice colleagues wanted to forgo the social science and research teaching. That is why (with ambivalence) they valued a university connection. Although the New York School had no formal Columbia connection until 1941, arrangements for cross-registration existed from the beginning and Columbia faculty members and others carried much of the academic side in the social work curriculum with social science training. Similar situations occurred in the other schools, either through earlier university affiliations or through other arrangements.

Zimbalist (1977) distinguishes between the monumental European poverty studies of Booth in London and Rountree in York in the late 19th century and the U.S. social research (especially Watson's compilations). The Americans, he believed, focused on measurements of poverty and the British focused on explorations of the causes of social problems. Both emanated from debate about Poor Law policy and the innovations of COS and settlements, however. And constant exchange of information and borrowing of program models occurred between the two countries (with Britain as the prime exemplar). Certainly the fact-finding and the considerable methodological innovation in these surveys were influenced by moralistic considerations (and, in the U.S., by Social Darwinist impulses). Nonetheless, the social work profession also had important roots in empirical social study of living conditions, household budgets, labor markets, housing, and disease as well as the histories of charity and reform.

It is not my intent to overstate the argument: Warner's (1894) collection of data and his interspersed morally anchored categories would not hold up in a modern dissertation defense. And the development of the casework method in the early decades of the 20th century depended on intelligent observation, insight, deduction from theory, and trial and error far more than on focused research. Nonetheless, the early social workers continued to attend to, consume, and occasionally contribute to social research. In the latter category, they focused on social conditions and populations. Years later, the first *Social Work Yearbook* (1929) spoke of "*social* research." In the 1937 *Yearbook* Helen Jeter insisted that *social work* research be differentiated. As the disciplines differentiated themselves, their social work explorations grew farther apart. Only in recent decades have social workers again pursued research that may also qualify as social science discipline-specific. A circle has been rounded and its full revolution should be considered in its implications for the social work research field.

Social Work Research as the Social Survey

In the decades following the birth of social work, society had become ever more conscious of the effects of industrialization, urbanization, and immigration. Some leading states would soon inaugurate new social protection policies such as workers' compensation and unemployment insurance. The federal government's role had begun to be reshaped. Poverty was being differentiated from pauperism. The new social science investigations and reports from social workers in the settlements and the COS had their impact (Bremmer, 1956). This period would later be described as the Progressive Era.

Earlier surveys of earnings and expenditures had been conducted in continental European cities and in England in connection with setting assistance levels, but Polansky (1975) notes the pioneering influences of the mid-19th century study of expenditures and budgets in Belgium by Frédéric LePlay. Another major influence was Charles Booth's *The Life and Labour of the People of London,* carried out between 1886 and 1907 and eventually published in 17 volumes related to poverty, industry, and religion. Booth had been motivated by the debate about Poor Law policy.

LePlay, Booth, and Rountree were part of the relevant context for what became the social survey movement in this country. The specifics are interesting because they belie some of the stereotypes about the COS. Early in the century (1905), the New York COS magazine *Charities* was joined with the settlement-derived *Chicago Commons* to become the premier social work journal of its time, *Charities and Commons.* Published by the New York COS, *Charities and Commons* was guided by a COS publication committee with members such as Jane Addams and Jacob Riis (Zimbalist, 1977). The publication's editor, Edward Devine, was general secretary of the New York COS and also was the first director of the New York School of Philanthropy when it launched a full one-year program in 1904. In the spirit of the age, special issues were devoted to such topics as "The Negro in the Cities of the North" and "Neglected Neighborhoods" (in the District of Columbia). Stimulated by the publication, a group of leading Pittsburgh citizens and social workers urged a study of social conditions in their city as part of the series. Paul Kellog, then on the magazine staff, was assigned the responsibility, and the new Russell Sage Foundation (1907) financed the study. The intent of the study was to disseminate information through journalism— not to produce science.

A "flying wedge" of investigators surveyed the local scene for six to eight weeks, followed by six consultants who devoted a year each to specialized monographs. Articles appeared in *Charities and Commons* in 1909, and the eventual product was 6 volumes and 35 articles (Zimbalist, 1977). Among the topics covered in this broadly conceived project were the following:

· wages, hours, and labor organization in the steel industry
· living conditions and household budgets
· industrial accidents
· trades employing women
· the economic costs of typhoid fever
· child-helping institutions and agencies in Pittsburgh.

Clearly, the public and the professions gained a valuable social analysis and a picture of the late 19th century industrial city and its problems and populations. There is evidence that the widely disseminated findings of one sub-study played a significant role in the success of the state workers' compensation movement before World War I. Social services were not emphasized. Zimbalist joins social science critics in the view that the survey was oriented to action, not the testing of hypotheses, and that the evaluation criteria were not objectified and sufficiently justified. In historical perspective, the Pittsburgh study represents a continuation and a refinement of the late 19th century social science, nonetheless—and a stage in a larger development. Evaluation concepts from the 1960s were not yet prevalent.

The Pittsburgh study of community needs had an extraordinary effect on other communities. More than 100 cities asked for surveys. The Russell Sage Foundation set up a survey department. The sponsoring magazine was renamed *The Survey,* and Kellog was to edit it for many years. By 1928 some 2,800 surveys were reported, especially surveys of education, health, and sanitation. Few were as comprehensive as the Pittsburgh study. By the late 1920s, enthusiasm waned as cities' responses to study results became less certain. More specialized federal and state statistical series provided new and valuable data. Sociology developed its discipline-based (and methodologically more rigorous) community studies related to its theory development.

By the time of Philip Klein's second Pittsburgh survey (Klein, 1938) the focus of the research was much narrower. The broader economic, social, and political overview was context; the heart of the survey was the study of social work "needs and resources." The many community surveys in the 1940s and 1950s, sponsored or carried out by community chests and councils or other social welfare agencies, focused on social welfare needs and were geared to planning and advocacy for program budgets. Community council researchers were among the founders of the Social Work Research Group (SWRG). And a social work research literature about needs still exists.

Russell Sage closed down its social survey department in 1931; the *Survey* magazine had become an excellent periodical covering social welfare and social work. It was not superseded by more specialized journals until 1952, when it ceased publication.

Social Work Research as Social Welfare Statistics and Social Indicators

It is no longer necessarily the case, but at an earlier time, people who assembled and analyzed agency and community statistics were identified as *social work researchers.* McMillen (1939) reports a comprehensive national effort. Zimbalist (1977), who cites McMillen, identifies the concentration on "statistics and index making" as one of his social work research "waves." Yet the activity is as old as professional social work and is not concentrated in any one time. Warner used COS and other statistical compilations at the turn of the century, as did many others. Nearly forty years later, in 1933, Philip Klein published *Some Basic Statistics in Social Work* using data from New York City family agency files. To Klein, this beginning look at the place of social work in the community by tabulating client contacts by geographic area as the economic depression developed was a "needs" study. Writing a dissertation under sociologist Robert McIver, Sophie M. Robison (1938) published the influential *Can Delinquency Be Measured?* raising major questions about differential reporting as affecting measurement of antisocial activity. These are but two of many illustrations.

This arena had and has considerable range: efforts to develop national private agency statistics; early census or census-like forays; the extraordinary work of Children's Bureau social workers as they developed research focused on the situation of children before there was acceptance of a federal social welfare program role; the special data collection for the several decennial White House Conferences on Children; and, finally, the experiments in index-making focused on dependency or social breakdown. A number of city-wide community chests and councils featured such work in their planning activities following World War II; since then, it has had periods of high activity from time to time in local and national organizations.

Nonetheless, even ambitious efforts within national voluntary associations (child welfare and family service, for example) at best produced administrative data oriented to programs. Such surveys could not provide cumulative client-related statistics. The gathering of this kind of data would depend on more ambitious undertakings by the U.S. Census Bureau and various mission agencies.

Governmental reporting improved enormously during the 1930s, as illustrated, for example, by *Recent Social Trends* (1935), a Hoover-administration initiative. Social work researchers rarely participated among the statisticians and demographers who took over. An exception was Mollie Orshansky of the Social Security Administration, who developed the conceptual strategy for what became the Census Bureau absolute poverty line, reported annually from the early 1960s to this day (Fisher, 1992). By the 1960s the social indicator movement was under way, and despite local work by social work researchers, the national efforts were led by the Social Science Research Council and the Russell Sage Foundation. By 1969 Wilbur Cohen, Secretary of the Department of Health, Education and Welfare had issued *Toward a Social Report.* There were several subsequent governmental social indicator compilations and most mission agencies (justice, health, education, public assistance, agriculture, housing, and so forth) now issue indicators in their fields. A Federal Interagency Forum on Child and Family Statistics recently issued a valuable compilation under the leadership of the Office of Management and Budget, *America's Children: Key National Indicators of Well-Being* (1997). The voluntary sector also remains active. The Annie E. Casey Foundation's *Kids Count*, and the Children's Defense Fund's *The State of America's Children Yearbook* serve as examples.

It seems fair to say that social workers, often social work researchers, are part of this work at the state and local level but seldom participate at the federal level, and that indicators are not a central preoccupation of social work researchers. Only one faculty member at a social work school (an economist) was among those invited when a Congressional committee commissioned the National Academy of Sciences to undertake a review of poverty measurements (Citro & Michael, 1995). The current movement to use social indicators to monitor the impacts of P.L. 104–193 (welfare reform) is not a social work initiative.

A measurement study of the 1950s that had considerable social work participation was the social breakdown research of Bradley Buell (1952) and his colleagues and the series of major studies (and even the casework text) that followed. While Buell's work was a "burst" of confined duration, it left social work with the concept of the *multiproblem* family, was a forebear of William Wilson's later *urban underclass* category, and could trace its history back to the Victorian concept of *deserving* and *undeserving* poor people.

Social Policy Research

Social surveys and social indicator work fall under the rubric of policy, but other important strands also contributed. The earlier discussion has suggested that the dual origins of early social work education, especially the role of the emerging social sciences (in the context of the Progressive Era), did not leave the COS movement oblivious to the economic and social environment and to social policy matters. Among the early lecturers at the COS-sponsored New York School of Philanthropy was Isaac M. Rubinow, a social insurance scholar and advocate who published *Social Insurance, with Special Reference to American Conditions* in 1913.

Nonetheless, the settlements were the primary early promoters of what would now be called social work policy research. One of the settlements' announced missions was to report to the larger society on the neighborhoods in which they had settled. Another mission was to advocate for improved living conditions. Despite exceptions, this commitment did not produce a significant volume of rigorous research (one exception cited by Zimbalist was the 1895 *Hull House Maps and Papers*). Nonetheless, the support for research remained, and data were used in policy advocacy. Chicago was an important center of activity in this regard. Austin (1986) reminds us that Julia Lathrop had worked at Hull House, taught research in the initial Chicago social work training program, and became the first chief of the U.S. Children's Bureau, initially largely a center for research on the condition of U.S. children. Grace Abbott, also from Hull House, continued the tradition of applying research data to policy advocacy. Austin quotes Edith Abbott, Grace's sister, as emphasizing a social work curriculum in which social policy was treated equally with public welfare administration. The University of Chicago established *The Social Service Review* as a vehicle for dissemination of social work research findings. In the early years, in particular, faculty from several social science departments taught the social work research courses at Chicago, as they did in many schools.

During the 1930s, with the sponsorship of the faculty of the University of Chicago School of Social Service Administration (which still publishes *The Social Service Review*) the University of Chicago Press produced a remarkable group of policy studies. Strong in their legal and social administration content, these publications were led by Grace Abbott's two-volume *Child and the State*, Sophonisba Breckinridge's *The Family and the State*, and *Public Welfare Administration in the United States*, as well as Edith Abbott's *Public Assistance* and *The Tenements of Chicago: 1908–1935*. The Chicago faculty members and their students also produced a valuable series of state "poor law" histories.

Social Work Research, Evaluation, and the Launching of SWRG

We note a series of converging phenomena in the late 1940s and early 1950s:

- social agency board members asking about the impacts of casework
- the height of the "psychiatric deluge" in social work practice and the beginning interest in alternative models, some of which involved social science concepts
- increased numbers of social workers with doctoral training, including rigorous social science training, on social work faculties and on the research staffs of councils of social agencies, community councils, and a few federal departments.

Later, the Russell Sage sponsorship of new social science concentrations in the doctoral programs at Michigan and Columbia and the grants to individual social scientists (Otto Pollack, Hope Leichter, Howard Polsky) to concentrate on social welfare-connected studies would further spur the formalization of social work research.

Social work researchers from several community councils, large family and children's agencies, social work schools, and federal agencies began with city-based luncheon clubs, exchanged views at national social welfare conferences, and finally, in 1948, launched the SWRG. All the other social workers had professional homes. The child welfare, public welfare, and family services staffs participated in the general American Association of Social Workers (1921) and in their respective national functional associations—the Child Welfare League of America (CWLA), Family Service Association of America (FSAA), and American Public Welfare Association (APWA). School social workers, medical social workers, and psychiatric social workers had long-since organized. The social group workers association came together in 1936 and the community organizers in 1946. With SWRG to complete the roster, the stage was set for the 1955 consolidation that created the National Association of Social Workers (NASW).

The launching of SWRG gave social work research a considerable boost, as did the program of what the NASW called its Research Section (Maas, 1977). Several key documents were produced on the function of social work research; a series of productive meetings was convened at the National Conferences of Social Welfare; there was a research section in NASW's initial journals; there were several mini-conferences, especially one on child welfare research in 1956; and the research section sponsored a first social work research text (Polansky, 1961).

What SWRG and Research Section members talked and wrote about most was social work evaluation. As put by David French (1952) in *An Approach to Measuring Results in Social Work* (his then-influential, since-forgotten book on measuring results in social work), board members from the Michigan Welfare League, his study sponsor, were constantly being asked, "Are people being benefited by social work services in the way they need to be benefited? Is the money which the community is investing in social work services producing results which justify continuing or extending their services? What kinds of improvements are possible in making social work services more effective?" (p. 14).

Gordon Allport, professor of psychology at Harvard, told a 1954 Columbia Bicentennial conference "the brightest feature of the present situation is the spirit of self-objectification, self-scrutiny and self-criticism that marks contemporary social services. Social workers are less inclined than formerly to mistake our good intentions for good results, our own professional growth for growth in our clients. Today the question is whether social services . . . do in fact achieve the results we claim to achieve" (Allport, 1955, p. 195).

Allport referred to earlier accomplishments and to the major work under way as he spoke. He cautioned against faddism in borrowing from partial knowledge in psychiatry, psychology, or medicine without recognizing their "unfinished state"—and without contributing out of social work materials and experiences to the rounding out and refining of the social sciences.

A hot topic at the time of SWRG's beginnings was the efforts of a sociologist, John Dollard, and a psychologist, O. Hobart Mowrer, to use content analysis of case records from the Community Service Society of New York. The final product was a curve showing the course of a Distress-Relief Quotient (DRQ) over the life of a case. While these prestigious researchers could show high reliability, ultimately their underlying assumptions were weak (Zimbalist, 1977).

Social work researchers apparently were judged ill-equipped to set a new course in evaluation. Although the "judges" and "raters" in the study by Dollard and Mowrer and the one that followed were social work practitioners, the Community Service Society (heir to the New York COS and sponsor of what became the Columbia University School of Social Work) engaged two eminent psychologists, J. McV. Hunt and Leonard Kogan, for its next efforts. These scholars developed a long-term commitment to the problem. What became known as the Hunt movement scale was a system of ratings based on judgments of readers of case records. The scale registered considerable reliability; and unlike the DRQ, it was compatible with social agency culture. The Hunt movement scale had enormous influence on the methodologies of casework research in subsequent decades. Still, critics noted that validity could not be shown by research limited to the case record. At best, the scale measured change in the context of treatment; given the lack of controls, the research could not identify the sources of change or its duration (Hunt & Kogan, 1950; Zimbalist, 1977).

Controls had been built into the earlier Cambridge-Somerville youth study, which has been described as an experiment in reducing delinquency through a program of preventive counseling (Powers & Witmer, 1951). The individual who conceived of and directed the youth study was a physician, Dr. Richard C. Cabot. At the end, neither delinquency records nor social adjustment measures showed differences between treatment and control groups. In a review at the time, this reader wondered whether the counseling was competent, standardized, or even social work (Kahn, 1952). In a brilliant subsequent reanalysis, Helen Witmer (1952) showed how a perceptive social work researcher could discern a good deal about who benefited from the counseling. In any case, as Zimbalist (1977) notes, the Cambridge-Somerville youth study did much to encourage a wide range of field experiments to measure effectiveness, an activity which persists. Subsequently the field experiment design was carried to welfare offices to test staffing levels, caseload sizes, and special interventions. Researchers and others paid particular attention to some of the latter work carried out by SWRG member Edward Schwarz in the Chicago Midway office. Schwarz was based in the research center at Chicago's School of Social Service Administration. Another line of evaluation during this period was launched by John Hill and Ralph Ornsby (1953; also Hill, 1960) as they brought systematic cost accounting to social work research.

Efforts to complete studies based on rigorously examined judgments or controlled experiments expanded during the 1950s and for a period thereafter. Space limitations do not permit specific citations. Polansky (1977) has sketched the pathway from this evaluative research to research into casework practice. A new type of practitioner-scholar worked on diagnostic categories, treatment conceptualizations, and analysis of the components of the intervention (for example, Ripple's [1964] studies of motivation, capacity, and opportunity). It was an optimistic time. New and better-trained social workers, educated in post–World War II doctoral programs, had joined the effort, which was no longer assigned largely to behavioral and social scientists from outside the field. Several academically based social work research centers now existed. The University of Chicago School of Social Service Administration dedicated its research center (1953) to casework research; the Columbia research center focused on delinquency, corrections, and the blind; and the Heller School at Brandeis pioneered in social planning conceptualizations, social service delivery research, and other policy areas.

The 1960s to the 1990s: Social Work Research as All of the Above, and Much More

Perhaps more time is needed for perspective. Or perhaps Zimbalist's notion of "waves" and "cycles" could not hold as modern social work became more extensive and its practitioners more specialized than the sum total suggested by its pre-NASW associations. And major developments in the role of government and in the behavioral and social sciences have affected social work and social research. While social surveys, social indicator work, and evaluation no longer can be said to dominate the field, each— particularly evaluation—remains an ongoing theme. And while no one note characterizes the 1960s, 1970s, or 1980s, much was going on and a variety of subthemes are identifiable.

The literature by now is vast, but some access to themes and trends is facilitated by three extremely valuable research reviews by Maas (1966, 1971, 1978), a related review of child welfare research (Norris & Wallace, 1965), and a sampling of articles in the *Social Work Yearbook* and the *Encyclopedia of Social Work*.[4] One finds not only themes and trends but also difficulty in classification; it is not easy to grasp this constantly growing profession.

In a sense, the child welfare research report and the Maas reviews are the direct results of the creation of SWRG and its successors, the Research Section and the Council on Social Work Research in NASW. The membership was interested in an evaluative analysis of social work research. The Research Council and the Child Welfare League sponsored an institute that was marked by two strategies: First, the child welfare to be talked about dealt mostly with actual or potential child-family separation (one could not at one time look at all aspects of child welfare). Second, the work of both practitioners and researchers would be acknowledged and the practitioner-researcher role would be encouraged as the social work counterpart of the clinical investigator in medicine. Child welfare was seen as an area in which social workers predominate, but bridge-building with the behavioral and social sciences was encouraged as, for example, in the major roles assigned anthropologist, psychologist, sociologist, psychiatrist, and pediatrician participants in child welfare research. Note was made of a need for child welfare personnel to take more notice of child development research, in itself an interdisciplinary field, and the likelihood that child development researchers would want to move into some child welfare research areas long considered social work domains. This, of course, has subsequently occurred on a major scale, while child development has made enormous strides since the early 1960s as a behavioral science. Most important, however, the child welfare research review described a complex arena of evaluative, organizational, staffing, process, and decision-making methodologies. It found "considerable variations in methodological acumen" (p. 67) and made available much experience and many insights that could upgrade methodology. It also dealt with issues in the institutionalization of child welfare research.

The Maas (1966) review summed up research in eight fields of service. It proved possible to follow the planned strategy for five fields, where "services [are] organized directly under social welfare auspices . . . family service, public welfare, child welfare, neighborhood centers, and social planning agencies" (p. 5). The three fields of social work where the institutional host is another profession proved elusive: corrections, medical social work, and psychiatric social work. (The reader will note, of course, how much currently funded social work research activity derives from two of these fields: the medical and the psychiatric). The resulting baseline reviews are excellent and need not be discussed further here except to note their range and the tendency of each review to require its own outline because of the varying concerns with populations in focus, types of problems, administrative loci of services, and the varied interventions. Each review generates a large agenda of issues and many valuable suggestions. One is impressed with the range and complexity of what has become social work research. Or *is* it all social work research? Certainly the referenced studies for some topics—especially public welfare, neighborhood centers, and planning—are interspersed with the names of many economists, sociologists, and social psychologists, often working in settings other than social work. Psychologists are especially well represented in other studies.

Maas intended to revisit and update these reviews "in the years ahead" and, in 1971, largely accomplished this. Two of his prior authors again contributed. The same five "fields" were covered. However, developments in the interim required that he "tack a social work *practice* approach onto the fields-of-service format" (Maas, 1978, p. 6). Thus, the family services chapter includes studies in casework, and the neighborhood center chapter contains a comprehensive review of research in group work. Instead of a chapter on social planning, there is a chapter on community organization (inevitable, one might comment, for social work in the Great Society).

The 1971 Maas review was valuable for researchers. Maas also made several observations relevant to our purposes. First, he noted that research into the phenomena of concern to the fields of childhood dependence, family or neighborhood organization, and poverty is undertaken and reported under a wide array of auspices and "appears in the publications of many scientific disciplines and practicing professions" (p. 7). Second, he observed, child welfare research had developed so extensively over the previous five years as to require the review author, Alfred Kadushin, to limit himself to child placement. Third, Maas reported, a serious problem existed in research utilization—or rather in the lack thereof by practitioners. Finally, Maas noted that he had used the "existing service packaging labels" as a way to communicate with social work colleagues but he wondered about his "potpourri of services, agencies, and practices" (p. 10). Would future reports offer guidance to service organization and policy development that was "effectively and humanistically responsive to individuals' social welfare wants" (p. 10)? Social work and social work research had become increasingly complex.

When Maas turned to his third review (1978), covering the period from 1970, he had to rethink his organizational scheme. The new programs, roles, and benefits of the Great Society had left a mark. Maas commented: " . . . in recent years, social work has shown a renewed interest in the use of a social-problem orientation, linked with a population-at-risk focus for specifying professional goals" (p. 6). Discarding what he had previously found to be unsatisfactory, Maas organized the 1978 review under selected categories of populations at risk: families, children in adoptive homes, children in foster families and institutions, troubled people (defined as "people with psychological incapacities for coping with their often overwhelming worlds"), and elderly people. He remained with the traditional social work clients of the era but acknowledged that poverty, race, and physical handicaps presented problems of overlap and difficult-to-isolate social work foci. We must note that Maas could report very little research on the "War on Poverty." Social workers in some places had been effective antipoverty activists, but there were no notable research products.

During the 1970s and 1980s, Congressional actions led to the creation of many small grant programs for demonstration and research projects related to specific social problem groups (for example: abuse and neglect, runaway youth, spouse abuse, delinquency diversion, special education for the handicapped, Head Start, and so forth). As a result, one would today offer a longer, more categorical, but also more fragmented list than the one Maas proposed. As time passes it becomes increasingly difficult to develop a logical typology for social work research following the schemes in any or all of his three reviews.

Maas did comment on another development that dates from an earlier time: the research concentrated more on how to help and less on problem etiology. Most social work scholarship has long regarded etiological research as the arena of the behavioral and social science disciplines. The exceptions have been cases in which social work researchers trained in the behavioral and social sciences have continued to work in those disciplines as well. We will return to the point.

Maas probably gave inadequate attention to the major role of federal research funding from the late 1960s, covering the whole range of social policy and thus including both areas with little social work presence and those with traditional social work involvement: Social Security, public assistance, food stamps, Women Infants and Children (WIC), work programs, abuse and neglect, service integration, technical innovation, child care, Head Start, immunization, and others. Now competing for resources, social work applicants did not always prevail in areas in which they believed they had a claim, and social work researchers showed preferences for some topic areas over others. However, the patterns were not readily summarized, leaving us with the question: what *is* the social work research domain?

Before the NASW social work encyclopedias there were the yearbooks, first produced by Russell Sage (1929 to 1949) and then published by the cooperating specialized social work professional associations (1951 to 1960). From the first (1965) edition, the *Encyclopedia of Social Work* has offered yet another observation point for social work research. A hint of what has been going on appears in the changing numbers of articles classified as covering social work research: one in 1965, four in 1977, eight in 1987, and thirteen in 1995. Depending on one's perspective, the field has become more specialized (or fragmented), methodologically differentiated, and perhaps embattled. Yet all the articles describe an active enterprise spanning many fields of practice, many social problem areas, and both sophisticated and relatively simple design and statistical manipulation.

The reported studies deal with clients, needs, problems, service delivery, effectiveness and impact, and additional topics. The major tendency is "to study phenomena through naturalistic methods; that is, without experimental manipulation" (Reid, 1995, p. 2041).

While such methods are obviously often appropriate, they are not appropriate for some purposes. Critics also have expressed concern about nonrepresentative samples and employment of statistical techniques when the research design does not sustain the implied assumptions (Reid, 1995, p. 2044).

In general, the theme articles in the encyclopedia series tend to be self-critical: The research is "relatively primitive" (Shyne, 1965, p. 763); "most of the knowledge used by social workers lacks a strong empirical base" (Reid, 1987, p. 474); "a hundred years of effort to construct a base of scientific knowledge for the profession has fallen short of the enthusiastic hope of the pioneers" (Reid, 1995, p. 2041), and "The amount and quality of research in social work are inadequate to meet the profession's need for knowledge" (Austin, 1991, p. 62). Research in social policy and administration tends to be treated in the relevant topical articles rather than in the research overviews.

New Notes and Discontent

Three new notes and some discontent appear in the most recent discussions, perhaps reflecting disappointed reactions to efforts in the 1950s, 1960s, and 1970s to measure the effectiveness of casework—and the ensuing debates. Or perhaps they reflect new thinking about how social work research might contribute more to practice. Robert Schilling offers a historical interpretation (personal communication, June 1997):

> To some extent, we have overplayed these debates. They were perhaps inevitable. Social work was a maturing profession, in which the "big building blocks" of theories/models of helping (virtually all rehashed from the sociobehavioral sciences, in my view) were in place by 1970. Micro theories, specialization, and quantitative methods of inquiry tend to become more important as a discipline/profession matures, and eventually, the original "building blocks" seem less important as points for heated discussion—but are seen as important in a historical context. One can look at psychology and sociology to see this to be true in other arenas, as well as social work. Thus, the debates of the 1970s began when folks started asking if the emperor had any clothes. The questions were asked, and the methods of science applied to social work, in the context of a many-decades-long western infatuation with science/technology and the fruits thereof. Inevitably, there would be those who, for many reasons, did not like such questions being asked, nor such methods being applied to social work. But it is necessary that we ask, and continually attempt to answer, the complex question: what works, for whom, under what conditions? If social workers do not ask such questions, others surely will; lacking data they will come to their own conclusions.

Recent developments are summarized below under the headings single-system design, intervention research, epistemology, and the social work research task.

SINGLE-SYSTEM DESIGN

Borrowed from the field of psychological research, this method (also recognized as *time series* research) has been of interest to some innovative professionals as more satisfactory in measuring effectiveness than broad experiments. To others it provides the basis for what is called *empirical practice.* I have noted such names as Tripodi, Briar, Blythe, and others in the lead (for references, see Bloom, 1993; Blythe, 1995; Reid, 1995). Reid (1995) offers a succinct description of the method:

> Data on a target behavior or problem collected before, during, and after intervention are used to form a profile of change over time. From this time series, one can assess if a change in the behavior or problem appears to be associated with the use of intervention. . . . Through various manipulations of the intervention . . . it is possible to achieve a high degree of control over the extraneous factors that may explain change. . . . (p. 2046)

Promoting such methods, the Council on Social Work Education required schools to prepare students "systematically to evaluate their own practice" (Reid, 1995). Thus far (my exploration is limited) the visible impact is apparently in the schools, not the agencies. The parts of the methods most adopted are goal specification and use of standardized instruments. No serious argument is made that the single-subject design can satisfy all the assessment needs for social work practice. Nonetheless, one wonders whether the progress of the empirical practice movement and its methodological guidelines may not serve social workers well, as the single-subject design is applied to current expectations in the new performance-based contracting and managed care regimes in behavioral health programs and in some child welfare systems.

INTERVENTION RESEARCH

This is another development since the debates of the 1970s. In an application of research and development (R&D) logic from the late 1980s, intervention researchers have said that they do not primarily seek knowledge (I assume that they mean in the behavioral or social science *basic* sense) and that their purpose is to develop and test interventions. Indeed, some researchers argue that intervention research is what social work knowledge building actually is—or should be. Here one notes work by Thomas, Rothman, Reid, Bailey-Dempsey, and others (cited in Reid, 1995; Rothman and Thomas edited a pioneering volume in 1994). Illustration can be found in the ongoing projects of Columbia's Social Intervention Group (SIG), a 50-person multidisciplinary team led by Robert Schilling and Nabila El-Bassel (Schilling, 1997 and interview).

The projects' points of departure generally are some of the most difficult social problems: AIDS, addiction, homelessness, domestic violence. The location of the work is not an agency office but the field setting: a hospital emergency room, a prison, a shelter for the homeless. In a sense, intervention research is best conceived as a program including several phases and methods, with full payoff coming only if the full sequence (summarized here in four stages) is followed:

1. Studies oriented to understanding a social problem, so that an intervention may be developed. The studies may focus on individuals experiencing the problem, practitioners, community people attempting to cope, organizations, or communities.
2. Studies aimed at designing an intervention, component by component, with testing as needed; pilot studies of the intervention.
3. A full-scale randomized field experiment, which could be multiyear.
4. Plans to incorporate findings into normal service settings. (One must recognize here the possibility of more modest studies addressed to components particularly strategic at a given time and place.)

The method is new, the problems tackled are among our most complex, and only a few comprehensive projects are under way. We have yet to learn whether social work will be the major host for such efforts (since it does not monopolize interest in the problems), whether funding and institutional auspices will be available, and whether the research creativity (invention of potent interventions) will be equal to the challenge. Surely social work is an appropriate host here; what more important tasks challenge a social work researcher? But who could argue against others, for what clearly requires multidisciplinary strategies?

EPISTEMOLOGY

It seems to me that the epistemology explosion was a reaction to the poor results of casework evaluation studies; in other words, it was a situation of attacking the messenger. But of course the debate is a serious one and one can ask whether traditional research models work when the objects of study are human beings and human behavior.

I cannot but observe that social work was born when the modern scientific paradigms began to be applied to the human condition and that modern social science, whatever its limitations, is not without major achievements. It never seemed likely that in its search for information, knowledge, and effective interventions, social work would fully forgo the rational strategies that built space shuttles, produced genetic engineering, and invented what it took to establish modern medicine. But this is not the place for that debate. I'm impressed with Reid's (1995) note that while "the controversy may have outlived its usefulness, it has encouraged careful methodological reassessments in social work research, has called for frameworks that favor 'diverse viewpoints', and given needed impetus to use of qualitative methods as appropriate" (p. 2045).

The Social Work Research Task

How can one summarize the evolving task of social work research? Writing in the first official social work research text, MacDonald (Polansky, 1960) began, "neither subject-matter nor method serves to define and delineate social work research. The idea of function is more useful. The function of social work research is to contribute to the development of a dependable body of knowledge to serve the goals and means of social work in all its ramifications" (p. 1). Writing in the *Encyclopedia of Social Work* (1965) a few years later, Shyne struck a similar note and added that both practitioner and research worker share the objective of improving social work practice. But it bears noting that when one adopts the function ("knowledge to serve the goals and means of social work . . . ") rather than the subject-matter and locus criteria promoted by Zimbalist (see above), one has described a field with very permeable boundaries and constantly changing preoccupations. Such research must be of varying degrees of generality (MacDonald, 1960). For example, *within* social work research people talk of the basic and the operational or applied studies, and their content may very well merge with that of basic social science.

WHERE IS THE PROBLEM—IF A PROBLEM THERE IS?

If one remains at an operational level, it is possible to sum up something of a consensus as to what social work research has become, is, does, or should do.[5] Social work research should (does) enrich understanding of individuals, families, groups, neighborhoods, communities, problems, policies, and programs with which social work *works*. (In this context *understanding* implies a diversity of things that will not be spelled out.) Social work research studies the effects and efficacy of interventions, and participates in the invention of new or improved case-level interventions or of public and private social policies. Social work research also should contribute to the counting, index-making, and indicator construction that are essential to social welfare administration, social accounting, planning, and reporting. All of these activities involve both descriptive and more analytic undertakings; they range from efforts to understand the world in fundamental ways to attempts to develop methodologies to control or to change phenomena. Some researchers subsume all of this under the rubric of expanding the social work knowledge base and thus contributing to practice; but it is also related to basic behavioral and social science theory and to administration and policy, topics that may not be conjured up by the term *practice*.

Although this is seldom said, brief consideration suggests that social workers and their research cannot limit themselves to a knowledge base for fields of practice in which social work is the major or host profession. Social workers in their largest numbers are employed in settings in which other professions are the hosts. Referred to as fields of practice, these settings include hospitals, schools, courts, clinics, neighborhood development corporations, army bases, private businesses, public employment offices, and more. The rationale is that social workers can bring special perspectives and skills to the missions of these institutions, developing interventions appropriate to the settings. Therefore, social work research must also be seen as contributing to understanding of client populations and institutional challenges that can go well beyond the confines of more narrowly defined social work knowledge for social work-led programs.

Beyond this, it can be argued that much social work research, if well anchored in the relevant behavioral and social science disciplines and their methodologies, could simultaneously contribute to the knowledge base and methodology of those specific disciplines.

In historical context, then, it seems reasonable to say that, despite periodic flashes or fashions or highlights, social work research interests have remained broad and additive (in the field of practice sense) even as the profession's practice concentrated on the micro and deserted much of its macro history in the 1980s and 1990s. But one should not ignore the periodic self-critical *Encyclopedia* articles (Shyne, 1965; Reid, 1995) or the Maas (1971) conclusions, also arrived at by others, as to the lack of research utilization by practitioners. This may be ascribed to deficits at either side of the research-practice relationship. Most recently, the NIMH task force (Austin, 1991) put the assessment this way: "Contributions of research in social work to the knowledge base of the profession and to *the knowledge base of other practice professions* are severely limited" (p. 16, italics added by author).

Where is the problem, if a problem it is? Social work is a practice-based profession whose leaders and educators certainly know that research education of its professionals is essential. At the very least, a profession prepares its practitioners to be research consumers and educates a research cadre. However, perhaps at least in part for lack of a supportive infrastructure and funding base, as the NIMH task force argued, the growth in the scope of social work's practice involvements has outstripped the expansion of its research interests and activities. Note the task force's summary of the present scope of social work practice settings: perinatal social work, gerontological social work, oncology social work, and psychiatric social work, all of which may be conceived as differentiations of medical or hospital social work. The task force also lists social workers as providing mental health services (presumably treatment, counseling, and rehabilitation) in psychiatric hospitals, community mental health centers, residential treatment centers, rehabilitation centers, and private practice. The report also lists social work staff roles in elementary and secondary schools (it could have added college counseling); neighborhood community development; immigrant and refugee programs; governmental and non-profit program administration; and public policy analysis. Elsewhere (referring to client groups) the report includes child welfare, income supports, drug and alcohol programs, HIV-AIDS, runaways, and homeless people.

The problem may be deeper than scope and infrastructure. All the definitions stress the role of research in discovering knowledge for practice. Yet Rosenthal (1992) was correct, even if her illustration is now outdated, in her claim that the "overall level of documentation of the knowledge assertions" in the major compilation of NASW policy statements "is rather low." Values, subjectively held beliefs, and undocumented factual assertions are characteristic. As much has been said for several decades about the state of knowledge for direct practice. Some among us are committed to improved knowledge building through formal research and dissemination; others resist formal research, stressing the art component of practice or (as noted earlier) questioning traditional research enterprises as vehicles for knowledge building.

On the one hand, some major administrative and policy studies may have encouraged policy shifts (permanency in child welfare, work programs in welfare, diversion in delinquency, open wards in psychiatric treatment); but at other times ideology and politics have been as potent or more so than research findings. Practice changes as often take their leads from the policy or program shifts and funding requirements as from trial and error, inspiration, demonstration, political correctness, and developments in the culture. Rarely do practice changes follow from fundamental research discoveries. The latter would have to be critical program evaluative studies in which both program and practice methods are shown to make a significant difference. Such studies are both difficult and scarce.

Most social work researchers do not conduct such studies because of both the resource-infrastructure requirements and because it is unclear just which studies need to be done. Here we must refer to the major deficits in research continuity in social work practice and other human services. When specialists read in their scientific journals of the latest breakthrough in cellular biology or astrophysics research, leading scholars in those fields identify the next challenges. Their science is being constructed brick upon brick. One knows where a next brick is needed—or at least can identify some possibilities. By their very nature, this is untrue of the base for social work practice or practice in the other human professions. Therefore, the researcher may take his or her problem not from a strategic approach to knowledge building but from locally and personally-defined priorities, or from what is at the moment attractive to public or private funding sources, or from priorities popular to topic-approving faculties in Ph.D. programs. Such results are seldom additive. Indeed, a distressing lack of continuity appears in federal and foundation research funding announcements, reflecting a failure to build one year's research priority announcements on the results of the awards of recent years. The exceptions are so rare as to be legendary, such as the heroic efforts of Charles Gershenson to promote research continuity and systematic knowledge-building in the research grant programs of the U.S. Children's Bureau during the 1970s. Thus, with neither practice nor research organized to inspire research continuity, the result is a repeating cycle in which the lack of compelling research findings allows much practice development to proceed unrelated to research.

Another element may improve this picture. SWRG began in 1948 to create a supportive community of research scholars, and the Society for Social Work and Research (SSWR) began in recent years and for similar reasons to work on building a stronger social work research infrastructure. However, the process also points to the estrangement of social work research and practice which can be aggravated by institutional separateness where this tendency is not guarded against. This separation is less common in the social and behavioral sciences, but it occurs in all human services and other direct practice professions. Austin (this volume) also has commented on this subject.

The aftermath of the 1991 NIMH task force and the subsequent creation of the Institute for the Advancement of Social Work Research has been an increase in NIMH support of social work research infrastructure and in NIMH research funding. Important early successes in giving social work research interests access to other federal supports have also occurred, as have some encouraging efforts to stimulate activity in social work education (Austin, this volume). But the problem may also reside in the failure of research to produce or disseminate compelling findings to which practice should respond. Moreover, the matter of research continuities and research utilization obviously will require further attention.

The social work profession is not organized as a learned society, nor should it be. NASW joins together the functions of experience-exchange and mutual support with important elements of politics and advocacy, enforcement of ethical standards, and some components of trade union-ism. Yet the profession's commitments and the urgency that practice and policy move forward on the soundest possible basis do require address. Austin (this volume) has properly called attention to the need to make annual meetings "a major showcase for significant knowledge-building and practice-relevant research" (p. 99). And NASW and the Council on Social Work Education are in a position to convene working groups or to commis-sion scholars to prepare practice assessments that highlight issues needing answers or clarification from research as the social work knowledge re-source is renewed. Scholars and their publishers now compete in offering alternative practice conceptualizations or alternative vocabularies for the conceptualizations. Can research offer any basis for selectivity?

It may also be necessary to explore further why there is no sense of urgency about these matters in much of the profession, and what else might be done. Does the social work profession need broader institutional reexamination of some fundamental questions about the profession, of how research is structured in relation to practice and education, and of the ways research responds to knowledge deficits? If researchers are separately organized, as they were in SWRG and are in SSWR, what disadvantages of such separation need to be overcome? If the professional association cannot include components of a learned society, how should research scholarship reach its constituencies?

Rounding the Circle, 100 Years Later

The needed reassessment must not ignore another fact of life—the extent to which social work has no monopoly in its described domains. Ours is a shared knowledge base, a shared program world, and a shared practice arena. (This sharing is, in fact, true to various degrees for all the major professions, medicine and education, for example).

OTHER PROFESSIONS, OTHER BEHAVIORAL AND SOCIAL SCIENCES

Many things very relevant to this discussion have occurred during the 100 years we have been exploring. In the first decade of the 20th century, American social welfare was a small enough enterprise to be left to the care and attention of the voluntary charities, the state boards, settlements, a few modern welfare departments, and the social workers. But even this reluctant society could not long resist what has become essential to all advanced industrial societies: the development of systems of social insurance, assistance, personal social services, and medical care on which the society depends for social protection against a diversity of risks. Public and private expenditures for social safety nets, treatment, rehabilitation, socialization, education and housing programs, development, help, and social control in the United States now total over one-third of the gross domestic product (Social Security Administration, 1997). While the programs originally were meant for poor people or for those outside the social mainstream, many major components of these packages are now universal. Although private charities and local government were once the main program providers, the federal government became central and the state and large private associations expanded their stakes. The social welfare world now encompasses more than what would be assigned to social work—even a professionalized and expanded social work—and more than what social work would claim as its domain. As it has grown, much of this world has became attractive to other professions and associations.

The social sciences, although differentiated from social work early in the century, never lost their involvement in the investigation of social problems.

In fact, there was never a clear break from the original pattern. As they grew and developed, the social sciences often attended to phenomena and trends of immediate concern to the broader society and to the social welfare field. Several social sciences developed *applied* streams. Further, in their own writings, the historians of the social sciences (for example, Sibley [1974] writing about the Social Science Research Council and Featherman [1991, 1994] updating that review) note how the needs of an era have shifted the balance for them between applied and basic disciplinary work. They illustrate with the New Deal, the post–World War II period, and the war on poverty. Thus, for example, since we have already referred to the University of Chicago social work contribution to policy research, in the 1920s and 1930s the University of Chicago sociology department sponsored many "now classic descriptive inquiries of human condition that stigmatize the person involved" (Maas, 1977, p. 1190): Neils Anderson, *The Hobo* (1923); Clifford Shaw, *The Jack Roller* (1930); Allison Davis, *Children of Bondage* (1940).

In their applications for funding, the disciplines have often departed from the case for adding to fundamental understanding of the world, instead calling attention to the societal significance of the issue or problem to be studied. Apart from the applied sociologists, economists, or social psychologists, other researchers have concentrated on the knowledge core of their disciplines but conducted what the Social Science Research Council in the 1990s came to call "mission-oriented basic research" (Featherman, 1991, p. 75):

> it is research in which practical concerns guide scientists' choice of topics. The research is conducted, however, in ways that do not necessarily yield immediate or directly foreseeable applications. (p. 75)

> The concept of mission oriented basic research describes much of what the social sciences . . . have done during this century. They have selected for attention issues, such as economic growth, the urban underclass, or international peace and security, that are high on the society's agenda. But they have not pursued these issues with an eye only on immediate policy concerns. . . . They have instead conducted research that has revealed deeper social and behavioral processes at work. (p. 75)

> But to do effective mission-oriented basic science we shall have to modify our commitment to the preeminence of disciplinary science. Mission-oriented research calls for interdisciplinary science and teams rather than individual-investigative models of scientific enterprise. (p. 77)

Beyond this, many economists develop careers not in basic disciplinary research but by using their field's knowledge in applied market, governmental, and nonprofit activity: the business, brokerage firm, or the bank; the Council of Economic Advisors, the World Bank, or the United Way, to cite a few examples. Political scientists become policy experts, political campaign consultants, or journalists reporting on national, state, or local politics.

Psychologists organize market research and marketing campaigns, advise on jury selection, or offer various consultant services to social service agencies and planners of retirement communities. This is only the beginning of a long list. It is offered as backdrop for the assertion that currently, as at no time since our beginnings a century ago, social work finds itself working alongside (or competing with, or fully superseded by) social scientists with regard to research and practice in social welfare. Obvious, clear, and accepted divisions of responsibility no longer lend themselves to a sharp delineation of the domain of social work research, unless one greatly narrows the current field of action.

OTHER PROFESSIONS, OTHER PRACTITIONERS

Social work's research mission is further complicated by the substantial development and expansion of other professional and occupational groups serving in the social services. In effect, the monopoly of the occupation assembled in the original National Conference on Charities and Corrections has long since ended. Social work lacks sanctions, legitimization or even fully acknowledged expertise with which to protect its roles where federal or state or accrediting body requirements or funding patterns do not protect it. Again, very early, corrections, city planning, public health, and what became social work went their separate ways (coming together in narrower collaborative and cooperative patterns over the years). More recently, since World War II, clinical psychology has grown beyond a testing and diagnostic discipline to become a therapeutic one. As such, clinical psychology now competes with social work in treatment roles. Most relief and refugee work turned largely to other disciplines during and after World War II. Public assistance agencies had fewer and fewer social workers on their staffs after the 1960s. As requirements were lowered for protective workers in child welfare, preprofessional human service graduates were deemed qualified. Currently a strong movement to accredit a youth development worker profession exists within the child welfare system, with no one asking where the social work group workers are. Few social workers are now found in the Washington bureaucracy where social security and public assistance analysis for policy development is done. Similarly, few social workers are found in some state bureaucracies (though not all) as they restructure public assistance programs under the 1996 legislation.

Other professions, occupational groups, and disciplines are actively at work in areas earlier claimed by social work or encompassed in the traditional formulation of the social work mission. Further, other professions, occupational groups, and disciplines have major research roles—and often *the* major research roles—in relation to the types of evaluation, invention of interventions, or general knowledge development long claimed by social work as its responsibility.

Social Work Research in a Pluralistic and Open System

Social workers, who conceive of their commitment as focusing on the person-in-environment, will know that their research roles must be conceived with regard to the profession in its broader institutional context. The earlier listing of activities and tasks for social work research assumed consensus within the profession as to our mission, and easy separation of our domain from other domains. In fact, the attempts to specify mission have been as elusive as the search for a unified conceptual framework. Social work is pulled in many directions by shifting and developing opportunities, the creativity of some of its innovators, the attractiveness of service opportunities and funding streams, and changing times. It is doubtful that this could be otherwise. Social workers are a motley crew in a pluralistic, dynamic social policy environment.

I therefore see no way to manufacture a template for social work research. However, there are other useful things to do. Maas has stressed the need somehow to accumulate "into bodies of knowledge useful to social work action what our studies have told us" (Maas, personal communication, 1998). The NIMH Task Force on Social Work Research (1991) has offered useful suggestions for capacity-building, for strengthening the research infrastructure of the profession (although it omits some important sectors). The Institute for the Advancement of Social Work Research has scored important early successes in opening doors and mobilizing resources. Specialized research associations, such as the Society for Social Work and Research, could help create vehicles for consideration of the challenges posed earlier: the need for broad institutional reexamination of some fundamental questions about the social work profession and how its research is initiated, structured, and disseminated in relation to knowledge deficits, practice, and education.

We may have rounded the circle again, in a sense: SWRG was launched in 1948, 50 years after the profession's beginnings, to support new directions in social work research. Now, after a stretch of integration and generic preoccupations, NASW is encouraging special interest groupings once again while other groups (such as SSWR) are self-organizing out from under the NASW umbrella. These groups may have a vantage point for playing a useful role in supporting a pluralistic research mission for social work that avoids control but encourages needed probing, development, and utilization.

Author's Note

This chapter, which had been prepared to commemorate the 50th anniversary of the founding of the Social Work Research Group (SWRG) in 1948, was originally to be titled, "Fifty Years of Social Work Research." As I began to deal with the subject, it seemed clear that it could be useful to consider as well the first 50 years of the social work profession, before 1948. My working title then became "1948 +/− 50," which translated eventually into the present title.

As a long-time teacher of the history of U.S. social policy, I consider a major function of the study of history to be the creation of a dialogue between the present and the past so as to stimulate and assist with current issues and concerns. I have so defined this undertaking. There is plenty of evidence that there indeed are issues and concerns about social work research: *What* is it? *Why* is it? *How* is it to be done?

I would like to make a few comments about my method. I have not carried out the comprehensive historical study of social work research that would give me undisputed license to lead off in the dialogue. However, I began to teach research and administer the M.S. thesis program at the New York School of Social Work in 1947, and continued there as a research teacher, eventually in the doctoral program, until the early 1960s when I elected to concentrate on theory and substance in social planning, policy analysis, and child and family policy. I was a member of the group that founded SWRG in 1948, attended several of its early conferences, and contributed a chapter to the first (1960) *Social Work Research* text edited by Polansky for the successor organization, the Social Work Research Section of the National Association of Social Workers (NASW). Later, as a member of NASW's Commission on Social Work Practice, and subsequently as its chair following Harriet Bartlett, I saw the research section become a council and then disappear with the disbanding of all the original special-interest groups during one of social work's generic periods.

To challenge my memory, I have reviewed Zimbalist's (1977) valuable history of social work research, which ends its story in the mid-1960s. Beyond that, I have relied on my observations at Columbia and other schools; direct experiences with policy and planning research; review of some (but hardly all) major sources (to which I refer); and interviews with a few generous colleagues and former colleagues.

Notes

1. (1) The Search for the Causes of Poverty (end of 19th century); (2) The Measurement of Poverty (early 20th century); (3) The Social Survey Movement (mostly pre–New Deal); (4) Statistics and Index Making (from the beginning and certainly since World War I); (5) Evaluative Research (the 1940s and 1950s); and (6) Multiproblem families (the 1950s).

2. See Kahn, A. J. (1998).
3. Required in the sense that these two books had become preparatory reading for the New York summer school in philanthropy by 1899.
4. The reader will understand that these, in turn, are the doorways to many critically important books and articles.
5. I use all of these terms in the remainder of this paragraph, without evaluative intent.

References

Allport, G. W. (1955). The limits of social service. In J. E. Russell (Ed.), *Natural policies for education, health, and social services* (pp. 194–213). New York: Doubleday.

Annie E. Casey Foundation (Annual). (1998). *Kids Count.* Baltimore: Author.

Austin, D. M. (1986). *A history of social work education.* Austin, Texas: School of Social Work, University of Texas.

Bloom, M. (Ed.). (1993). *Single system designs in the social services.* New York: Haworth Press.

Blythe, B. J. (1995). Single system design. In *Encyclopedia of social work* (19th ed., pp. 2164–2168). Washington, DC: National Association of Social Workers.

Bremmer, R. (1956). *From the depths: The discovery of poverty in the United States.* New York: New York University Press.

Broadhurst, B. P. (1971). *Social thought, social practice and social work education: Sanborn, Ely, Warner, Richmond.* Unpublished doctoral dissertation, Columbia University School of Social Work.

Bruno, F. (1948). *Trends in social work, 1874–1946.* New York: Columbia University Press.

Bruno, F. (1957). *Trends in social work, 1874–1956* (2nd ed.). New York: Columbia University Press.

Buell, B. (1952). *Community planning for human services.* New York: Columbia University Press.

Children's Defense Fund. (Annual). *The state of America's children yearbook.* Washington, DC: Author.

Citro, C., & Michael, R. T. (Eds.). (1995). *Measuring poverty: A new approach.* Washington, DC: National Academy Press.

Department of Health, Education, and Welfare. (1969). *Toward a social report.* Washington, DC: Author.

Encyclopedia of social work. (15th ed.). (1965). New York: National Association of Social Workers.

Encyclopedia of social work. (17th ed.). (1977). Washington, DC: National Association of Social Workers.

Encyclopedia of social work. (18th ed.). (1987). Washington, DC: National Association of Social Workers.

Encyclopedia of social work. (19th ed.). (1995). Washington, DC: National Association of Social Workers.

Featherman, D. L. (1991). Mission-oriented basic research. *Items, 45,* 75–77. New York: Social Science Research Council.

Featherman, D. L. (1994). SSRC, then and now. *Items, 48,* 13–22. New York: Social Science Research Council.

Federal Interagency Forum on Child and Family Statistics. (1997). *America's children: Key national indicators of well-being.* Washington, DC: Author.

Fisher, G. M. (1992). The development and history of poverty thresholds. *Social Security Bulletin, 55,* 3–14.

Fischer, J. (1973). Is casework effective? A review. *Social Work, 18,* 5–20.

French, D. G. (1952). *An approach to measuring results in social work.* New York: Columbia University Press.

Hill, J. G. (1960). Cost analysis of social work service. In N. A. Polansky (Ed.), *Social work research* (pp. 223–246). Chicago: University of Chicago Press.

Hill, J. G., & Ormsby, R. (1953). *Cost analysis method for casework agencies*. Philadelphia: Family Service Association of Philadelphia.

Hull House. (1895). *Hull House maps and papers: A presentation of nationalities and wages in a congested district of Chicago*. Chicago: Author.

Hunt, J. M., & Kogan, L. S. (1950). *Measuring results in social casework: A manual on judging movement*. New York: Family Service Association of America.

Kahn, A. J. (1952). Analysis of methodology in "Unraveling juvenile delinquency". In D. French (Ed.), *An approach to measuring results in social work* (pp. 161–172). New York: Columbia University Press.

Kahn, A. J. (1998). *Themes for a history: The first hundred years of the Columbia University School of Social Work*. Publication pending.

Kellog, P. U. (1914). *The Pittsburgh survey* (Vol. I). New York: Survey Associates.

Klein, P. (1933). *Some basic statistics in social work*. New York: Columbia University Press.

Klein, P., et al. (1938). *A social study of Pittsburgh: Community problems and social services of Allegheny County*. New York: Columbia University Press.

Maas, H. S. (Ed.). (1966). *Five fields of social service: Reviews of research*. New York: National Association of Social Workers.

Maas, H. S. (Ed.). (1971). *Research in the social services: A five-year review*. New York: National Association of Social Workers.

Maas, H. S. (1977). Research in social work. In *Encyclopedia of social work* (17th ed., pp. 1206–1213). Washington, DC: National Association of Social Workers.

Maas, H. S. (Ed.). (1978). *Social service research: Reviews of studies*. Washington, DC: National Association of Social Workers.

McMillen, A. W. (1939). *Measurement in social work: A statistical problem in family and child welfare and allied fields*. Chicago: University of Chicago Press.

Norris, M., & Wallace. B. (1965). *The known and the unknown in child welfare research: An appraisal*. New York: Child Welfare League of America and National Association of Social Workers.

Polansky, N. A. (Ed.). (1960). *Social work research*. Chicago: University of Chicago Press.

Polansky, N. A. (Ed.). (1975). *Social work research: Methods for the helping profession*. Chicago: University of Chicago Press.

Polansky, N. A. (1977). Research in social work: Social treatment. In *Encyclopedia of social work* (17th ed., pp. 1206–1213). Washington, DC: National Association of Social Workers.

Powers, E., & Witmer, H. (1951). *An experiment in the prevention of delinquency: The Cambridge-Somerville youth study*. New York: Columbia University Press.

Recent social trends. (1935). Washington, DC: U.S. Government Printing Office.

Reid, W. J. (1987). Research in social work. In *Encyclopedia of social work* (18th ed., pp. 474–487). Washington, DC: National Association of Social Workers.

Reid, W. J. (1995). Research overview. In *Encyclopedia of social work* (19th ed., pp. 2040–2054). Washington, DC: National Association of Social Workers.

Richmond, M. (1899). *Friendly visiting among the poor*. New York: Macmillan.

Richmond, M. (1917). *Social diagnosis*. New York: Russell Sage Foundation.

Ripple, L., et al. (1964). *Motivation, capacity, and opportunity: Studies in casework theory and practice*. Chicago: University of Chicago, School of Social Service Administration.

Robison, S. M. (1936). *Can delinquency be measured?* New York: Columbia University Press.

Rosenthal, B. S. (1992). Does the social work profession value research-based knowledge as a basis for social policy? *Areté, 17,* 38–46.

Rothman, J., & Thomas, E. J. (Eds.). (1994). *Intervention research: Design and development for human service*. New York: Haworth Press.

Rubin, A., & Gibelman, M. (1984). *Social work research in mental health*. Rockville, MD: National Institute of Mental Health.

Rubinow, I. M. (1913). *Social insurance, with special reference to American conditions.* New York: Henry Holt.

Schilling, R. F. (1997). Developing intervention research programs in social work. *Social Work Research, 21,* 173–180.

Shyne, A. W. (1965). Social work research. In *Encyclopedia of social work* (15th ed., pp. 763–773). New York: National Association of Social Workers.

Sibley, E. (1974). *Social Science Research Council: The first fifty years.* New York: Social Science Research Council.

Social Security Administration. (1997). *Annual statistical supplement to the social security bulletin.* Washington, DC: Author.

Social work yearbook. (1929). New York: Russell Sage Foundation.

Social work yearbook. (1937). New York: Russell Sage Foundation.

Task Force on Social Work Research. (1991). *Building social work knowledge for effective services and policies: A plan for research development.* Austin, Texas: University of Texas, School of Social Work.

Voiland, A. (1962). *Family casework diagnosis.* New York: Columbia University Press.

Warner, A. (1894). *American charities.* New York: Thomas Y. Crowell and Co.

Witmer, H. (1952). An analysis of "An experiment in the prevention of delinquency". In D. French (Ed.), *An approach to measuring results in social work* (pp. 155–160). New York: Columbia University Press.

Zimbalist, S. E. (1977). *Historical themes in social welfare research.* New York: Harper & Row.

CHAPTER 2

Social Work Research and the Quest for Effective Practice

Aaron Rosen, Enola K. Proctor,
and Marlys M. Staudt

Social work has long been concerned with strengthening the extent to which its research is capable of informing and guiding practice (see Greenwood, 1957; Kadushin, 1959; Kane, 1982). Over the years increasing attention has been directed toward this purpose. This attention resulted in the founding in the 1970s of the first two journals dedicated to publishing research (*Social Work Research & Abstracts* and the *Journal of Social Service Research*) and the founding about 20 years later of a journal dedicated to research on practice (*Research on Social Work Practice*). These advances notwithstanding, concern persists that social work researchers are not meeting the needs of practitioners. Such concern was reflected in the convening of a symposium in 1996 on psychosocial intervention research, cosponsored by the Institute for the Advancement of Social Work Research and the Office of Behavioral and Social Sciences Research at the National Institutes of Health, as well as in the publication of a special issue on intervention research in the journal *Social Work Research* (September 1997).

Emanating from similar concerns, this article reviews current publications in social work and assesses their potential in contributing to a body of knowledge of effective interventions. This review is based on the premise that social work practice must adhere to and be guided by effectiveness criteria. That is, interventions should be selected and used on the basis of

This chapter was originally published in the March 1999 issue of *Social Work Research*, Vol. 23, pp. 4–14.

The preparation of this chapter was supported in part by the Center for Mental Health Services Research (NIMH Grant MH50857) and by a faculty research award from the George Warren Brown School of Social Work. An earlier version of this chapter was presented at "Research for Social Work Practice: An International Conference," North Miami, Florida, January 26, 1998.

their empirically demonstrated effectiveness. Because journal publications are a major vehicle for accumulating and disseminating professional knowledge, they constitute a primary source of guidance for practice. Accordingly, we examined the current research published in social work journals in relation to its potential for contributing to effective practice.

Purpose of Professional Knowledge

The premise that intervention should be based on relevant and valid knowledge is at the core of professional practice. Rosen (1978, 1996) has conceptualized the knowledge needs of practice as related to the purposes for which knowledge is used and its function in practice. Three types of knowledge were distinguished: descriptive, explanatory, and control. Descriptive knowledge guides practitioners in classifying phenomena they encounter into meaningful conceptual categories. Often it is used by practitioners in deciding whether and to what extent a particular manifestation or event should be of concern—that is, considered a problem. Descriptive knowledge includes information on the characteristics, indicators, or incidences of phenomena of professional concern (for example, poverty, child abuse, maladaptive behavior, mental disorders, and community violence). Descriptive knowledge, in articulation with its values, also helps to formulate social work's objectives (Rosen, 1978), informs policy decisions about which services are needed by which client groups, and aids practitioners in assessing and classifying clients and problems into professionally meaningful categories. Explanatory knowledge is knowledge that provides insight into and understanding of the phenomena of concern—their dynamics, factors influencing their variability, and their consequences. It alerts practitioners to factors that probably contribute to the development and persistence of problems, and most important it provides practitioners with the basis for predicting the type and extent of other undesirable conditions likely associated with problems. Understanding of such dynamics guides practitioners' decisions about whether intervention is needed and toward which outcomes it is indicated. The third purpose for which knowledge is used in practice is to enhance practitioners' ability to control a phenomenon of concern—that is, the ability to change it (ameliorative function) or maintain its desired course (preventive function). Knowledge fulfills its control functions when it is capable of guiding practitioners in the selection and implementation of interventions that successfully attain the desired outcomes.

To discharge their responsibility fully with regard to any case or client, practitioners must rely on knowledge that has been tested and validated in relation to the function it serves—descriptive, explanatory, or control. Descriptive and explanatory knowledge are required for practice tasks of assessing, explaining, or anticipating the course of naturally occurring events (including those viewed as problems)—that is, providing ex post facto explanations regarding antecedent factors or predicting the naturally occurring consequences of the events. Performing these practice tasks involves passive predictions: The practitioner's role is a passive one in relation to the occurrence of the predicted event (Rosen, 1993). A critical junction in knowledge needs occurs when, based on passive prediction, a practitioner decides that intervention toward some outcome is indicated. At that point the practitioner must rely on control-capable knowledge to guide the selection of interventions and their implementation. Practitioners also change their mode of operation from passive to active prediction at that point. They no longer predict the natural consequence of an event or process, but rather predict the consequences (outcomes) of their own interventions, and their activities are deliberately designed to confirm the prediction. The attainment of desired outcomes, then, is a consequence of practitioners' action (see Rosen, 1993, 1996). To bring a practice episode (treatment) to a successful conclusion, practitioners must have and use valid knowledge capable of guiding both passive and active predictions.

An example from the field of mental health may further illustrate the functions of descriptive, explanatory, and control knowledge in practice, as well as underscore the distinction between passive and active prediction. A recently divorced client seeks help for insomnia, irritability, and loss of appetite. Based on these complaints and the client's Beck Depression Inventory (Beck, Ward, Mendelson, Mock, & Erbaugh, 1961) score, the social worker concludes that the client is depressed. In making this diagnosis the social worker was using descriptive knowledge that guided the classification of the client by professionally meaningful concepts (diagnosis) by viewing the client's characteristics in relation to population base rates and norms. Using explanatory knowledge the social worker formulated a hypothesis that the divorce likely precipitated the client's depression and that the client's condition would deteriorate unless treated (passive predictions). Thus, the social worker used descriptive knowledge for diagnosis and explanatory knowledge in assessment and for deciding that treatment was indicated. The social worker is in need of control knowledge to undertake treatment. Control knowledge would guide the social worker in the choice of an effective intervention (for example, cognitive–behavioral intervention) as well as in the implementation of the intervention's specific activities. Unlike explanatory knowledge, control knowledge deals with active prediction: The social worker's deliberate activities will bring about the predicted outcomes.

Unfortunately, the distinction between and different knowledge requirements of passive and active prediction tasks in practice often are overlooked. Failing to make such distinctions also may be coupled with the assumption (often implicit) that the ability to explain a phenomenon (passive prediction) is sufficient for being able to control it. These failures and assumptions, in turn, are likely to result in a disproportionate emphasis by social work researchers on research aimed at descriptive and explanatory knowledge at the expense of research directed specifically to production of control-capable knowledge (Rosen, 1996).

An appreciable part of the descriptive and explanatory knowledge essential for practice has been produced by the social sciences, in which explanation is the ultimate knowledge objective (see Kerlinger, 1986). In contrast, production of control knowledge aimed at influencing and changing events traditionally has been the domain and responsibility of the professions, as it is in social work (Rosen, 1978, 1996). A report of the Task Force on Social Work Research (1991) similarly observed, "There is a substantial body of social, behavioral, and biological research on many of the underlying causes of the human problems social workers address. But there are many gaps in our knowledge about 'what works'—that is, about the most effective . . . means of helping" (p. 4). Social work's disproportionate emphasis on descriptive and explanatory knowledge perhaps is sustained further by unwitting and indiscriminate adherence to the knowledge purposes and priorities of the social sciences, which occurs as a gratuitous appendage to social work's necessary use of social science's substantive and methodological contributions.

Ours have been among the voices that for some time urged social work researchers to intensify efforts toward the production of control-capable knowledge, and we also conceptualized the treatment process to facilitate such research (Rosen & Proctor, 1978, 1981; Rosen, Proctor, & Livne, 1985). Now it is our intent to examine research produced in social work in terms of the relative emphasis on descriptive, explanatory, and control knowledge and to assess the adequacy of control knowledge in informing practitioners' active predictions and guiding of interventions.

Requirements of Research to Guide Practice
CONTROL-CAPABLE KNOWLEDGE

Two decades ago we outlined the basic features of research that would produce professionally adequate, control-capable knowledge (Rosen & Proctor, 1978). We are convinced of the continued importance of these features and cite them as the assumptive context guiding this review:

· Knowledge regarding interpersonal treatment should enable practitioners to select and employ consistently an interventive approach that is relevant for a client and his/her presenting problem and situation, and which has been found to be effective for the desired outcome. Such knowledge should contain concepts that refer to behaviors that can be volitionally manipulated and systematically varied within the treatment process, and which are capable of reliable enactment across different helping situations. To meet these requirements, concepts and variables must be clearly defined and linked to empirical referents.

· Statements of interventive knowledge must also contain explicit predictions of the relationship between the interventive inputs and the desired outcomes. Interventive statements of this nature serve two indispensable functions: (a) they facilitate deliberate selection by practitioners of a given interventive approach from a number of possible alternatives on the basis of its applicability to a particular situation and treatment goal; and (b) they provide the framework within which their empirical validity can be tested—that is, they enable researchers to design studies in which the effectiveness of the interventive hypotheses can be rigorously investigated. (Rosen & Proctor, 1978, pp. 25–26)

These criteria must be met if studies of intervention are to contribute meaningfully to knowledge capable of guiding practice. Of these criteria, two basic ones will be used for classifying current research on intervention: (1) whether the interventions—the independent variables or treatments—are empirically denotable and can be reliably enacted by practitioners (these features would enable implementation of interventions with integrity [Yeaton & Sechrest, 1981] and, hence, replication in subsequent studies and in practice) and (2) the extent to which the outcomes against which the effectiveness of interventions is assessed were measured with sufficient specificity to allow reliable replication.

INTERMEDIATE AND ULTIMATE OUTCOMES

The utility of differentiating treatment outcomes as intermediate or ultimate, depending on the specific role they have in a particular treatment effort, has been advocated for researchers and practitioners alike (Nelsen, 1984; Rosen & Proctor, 1978, 1981). Whereas attainment of ultimate outcomes denotes the extent to which the treatment effort was successful in reaching its goals, intermediate outcomes are those deemed to be necessary preconditions or facilitators of the ultimate outcomes (Rosen & Proctor, 1978, 1981). Studies focusing on the efficacy of interventions legitimately may target either intermediate or ultimate outcomes. However, when the evaluation effort concerns the extent to which client problems were addressed successfully through an interventive program, ultimate outcomes must be included as dependent variables (Rosen & Proctor, 1978). To assess the relative emphasis placed in current research on intermediate and ultimate outcomes, we have differentiated outcomes by their role in the particular treatment effort that was investigated.

There have been several efforts in recent years to assess from a variety of perspectives the state of empirical research in social work. All efforts relied on publications in selected subsets of professional journals. Some studies were restricted to social work publications or to social worker authors, whereas others also included journals and authors from allied fields (see Fraser, Taylor, Jackson, & O'Jack, 1991; Glisson, 1995; Gorey, 1996; Klein &

Bloom, 1994; Lindsey & Kirk, 1992; Tolman & Molidor, 1994; Tripodi, 1984). As a group these reviews are informative, and each highlights a set of concerns with social work's knowledge development efforts.

The focus in our assessment concerned whether current research efforts appropriately address the different knowledge needs for effective and accountable practice, and our review in this article is guided by the perspective outlined previously. Accordingly, we analyzed publications in social work journals to assess the relative emphasis in social work research on generating descriptive, explanatory, and control-capable knowledge; the potential of control-oriented studies to contribute to a cumulative body of knowledge on the effectiveness of professional interventions (this was assessed from the perspectives of the replicability of the interventions studied and the specificity of outcome measurements); and the relationship between replicability of interventions and the specificity of outcome measurements.

Method
SAMPLE AND PROCEDURE

Although we did not set out to conduct an exhaustive review of social work publications, we selected our journals and a sample publication period to represent reasonably the primary current thrusts in social work research. Accordingly, we restricted our sample time frame to the most recent published work—between January 1993 and July 1997. We selected the journal sample by the following three criteria: (1) published in the United States expressly for or by social workers, (2) high likelihood of a preponderance of articles aimed at some aspect of social work practice (thus excluding journals such as *Journal of Education for Social Work*), and (3) likelihood of containing empirical studies of social work practice (in terms of publication history). Admittedly, these criteria may have excluded some highly relevant content, such as research published by social workers in non–social work journals or in social work journals not selected, research published only in books, or unpublished research. But we believe that our journal sample represents well those social work publications most likely to report control-oriented studies of interventions and most likely to be perused by social workers.

There was an appreciable overlap between our journal sample and those of previous reviews (Table 2.1). Of the journals included in the earlier studies, all that met our selection criteria also were included in our sample. The 13 journals were reviewed issue by issue, and all published articles were read and classified as either research or nonresearch. Excluded from this classification were editorials, book reviews, letters to the editor, brief notes, exchanges between authors, practice notes, commentary on current issues, and so forth.

Table 2.1. Social Work Journals Included in Current Study and Their Inclusion in Other Reviews

Journals in Current Study (n = 13)	Inclusion in Other Studies					
	Glisson 1995 (n = 5)	Fraser et al. 1991a (n = 10)	Tolman & Molidor 1994 (n = 9)	Gorey 1996 (n = 13)	Tripodi 1984 (n = 6)	Lindsey & Kirk 1992 (n = 19)
Administration in Social Work		X				X
Child & Adolescent Social Work Journal		X				X
Child Welfare		X	X		X	X
Families in Society		X	X		X	X
Health & Social Work		X	X	X		X
Journal of Gerontological Social Work		X				X
Journal of Social Service Research	X		X	X	X	
Research on Social Work Practice				X		
Social Service Review	X		X	X	X	X
Social Work	X		X	X	X	X
Social Work with Groups		X	X			X
Social Work Research	X		X	X	X	X
Social Work in Education		X	X	X		
Journals in common	4	8	9	7	6	10

aFor Fraser et al. (1991), we considered only the journals added to the original Glisson (1995) sample.

CLASSIFICATION OF ARTICLES

Research versus Nonresearch. An article was classified as a research article if it contained some of the components usually found in reports of research, such as a rationale for the study, questions for investigation, a systematically described methodology and data-gathering procedure, and a report of findings. If some of these components were missing, yet the author referred to the article as a report of a research study and presented original findings, the article was classified as research. Reports on single-system studies were included as research articles, as were systematically conducted meta-analyses of prior research. Nonsystematic reviews or syntheses of the literature, narrative-only case reports, and articles dealing only with research methodology without a substantive focus were not considered research articles. Following this classification all nonresearch articles were excluded from further analysis.

Classification of Research Articles by Knowledge Purpose. The research articles were classified by whether they addressed descriptive, explanatory, or control purposes, according to the primary thrust of the research study being reported. The following definitions guided this classification:

· Descriptive—Studies assessing the central tendencies or distribution characteristics of single variables, either in one population or sample or in comparisons across a number of populations or samples, were classified as descriptive. Also included in this category were studies aiming to conceptualize relevant variables (often qualitative in methodology). All studies meeting these criteria were included in this classification, irrespective of the rigor or other features of their design or their substantive focus.

· Explanatory—Articles reporting studies that investigated relationships (whether causal or not) among two or more variables were classified as explanatory. Hypothesis-driven investigations of differences between groups and multivariate explorations were classified as explanatory. These criteria were used regardless of the design of the study (for example, exploratory or experimental), the adequacy and rigor of the design, or the topic investigated.

· Control—Articles were classified as control studies if they investigated the effects of services rendered or if they tested the efficacy or effectiveness of interventions (for a discussion of efficacy and effectiveness, see, for example, Chambless & Hollon, 1998). Studies of practice at any level of analysis or type of intervention were included: helping approaches, treatment procedures, policy changes, or organizational implementation of service mandates or procedures. The type of the design (for example, single-system designs, clinical trials, and field experiments) and the adequacy of the design were not criteria for this classification. To be classified as a control study, it was necessary and sufficient that at least one of the interventions mentioned (of any form or level) was investigated in relation to one or more service outcomes. Thus, studies of curriculum changes or training procedures were excluded. Studies assessing effects of client-focused educational programs (for example, psychoeducation, parenting, and skills training) were included in this category.

If an article addressed descriptive and explanatory knowledge, it was classified as explanatory. Articles reporting control studies were classified as such, whether or not the studies also addressed knowledge for other purposes (descriptive or explanatory).

Classification of Control Studies. After articles were classified by their knowledge purpose, only the studies addressing control issues—those investigating interventions in relation to outcomes—were studied further. We assessed these articles according to a single criterion: whether the descriptions or definitions of the interventions investigated were specific enough to permit reliable replication of the intervention. Each of the interventions investigated in a given study was classified as replicable or nonreplicable. We decided to use replicability of the interventions as the single criterion in assessing control studies, because we view it as the most necessary and irreplaceable feature in the design of studies whose primary purpose is determining the effectiveness of interventions. Unless the interventions can be replicated with minimal error in subsequent studies and enacted with integrity in actual practice, the study's intended contribution to control knowledge is seriously compromised, regardless of other features of its design (for example, adequacy of controlling for alternative hypotheses and adequacy of sampling) or its findings. Because studies can investigate more than one intervention, a study was categorized as replicable if at least one intervention was classified as such. A study was categorized as nonreplicable if all interventions investigated were nonreplicable. The following operational definitions guided classification of interventions as replicable or nonreplicable:

- Replicable—An intervention was classified as replicable when it was described in sufficient detail to enable its implementation with integrity by a practitioner not involved in the study. Specifically, we judged as replicable interventions for which the investigators detailed the operational definitions or described precise practitioner activities. If the published report did not itself contain a detailed, sufficiently specific description of the intervention but included references to an available or previously published specific description or to a treatment manual, the intervention was classified as replicable. Interventions with available audio or video guides also were classified as replicable.
- Nonreplicable—Interventions not meeting the replicability criteria were classified as nonreplicable. These included interventions described only by a label (for example, "discharge planning," "systems approach," "cognitive–behavioral," or "family preservation") and interventions with no reference provided to specific, replicable definitions for such labels.

CLASSIFICATION OF OUTCOMES

Outcomes were classified in terms of two dimensions: (1) their role as intermediate or ultimate outcomes in a particular study and (2) the specificity of their measurement.

Role of Outcomes. Each of the outcomes was classified according to the role it had in the particular treatment being studied, whether the outcome was at the macro or micro level. The following definitions and decision rules guided this classification.

- Ultimate outcomes—Ultimate outcomes were defined as those treatment goals toward which treatment was undertaken and whose attainment rendered treatment successful.
- Intermediate outcomes—Intermediate outcomes were those pursued in treatment because they were seen as necessary or facilitative preconditions for attainment of other outcomes. (Rosen & Proctor, 1978)

If an investigator indicated an outcome as intermediate or ultimate, it was classified as indicated. If the role of an outcome was not explicitly indicated, clinical and service outcomes (for example, self-esteem, placement in foster care, and level of stress) and policy outcomes (for example, a board's reaching a decision) were classified as ultimate. Treatment process–related outcomes such as client satisfaction and attendance at treatment sessions were classified as intermediate outcomes. However, the context and the purpose of treatment also were considered in the classification of outcomes. For example, if compliance with a drug regimen was assessed as an outcome in a study evaluating the effectiveness of case management in reducing rehospitalization rates, compliance was classified as an intermediate outcome and incidence of rehospitalization as an ultimate outcome. If in that study compliance was the only outcome assessed in relation to case management, however, compliance was classified as an ultimate outcome.

Specificity of Outcome Measurement. The specificity with which outcomes were measured was used as an indicator of replicability of the measures. Determination of measurement specificity was based on the reported measurement procedure. Outcome measures were classified as having high, medium, or low specificity:

- High specificity—all standardized tests; measurements based on archival records of events and data of a very specific nature (for example, drug use test results, glucose levels, and recidivism rate)
- Medium specificity—nonstandardized rating scales, whether used by clients, workers, or researchers (for example, satisfaction, improvement, and goal attainment); definition-guided observations (for example, client behavior record)
- Low specificity—unguided observations or content analyses; self-reports.

RELIABILITY

The operational definitions and coding procedures were developed by the investigators based on the conceptual meaning of the variables being studied and on their measurement in previous research (see Mutschler & Rosen, 1979; Proctor & Rosen, 1983; Rosen & Proctor, 1978; Rosen, Proctor, Morrow-Howell, & Staudt, 1995). The actual classification was undertaken after a period of coder training, which included preliminary reliability trials and discussion of its results. Reliability was assessed on separate subsamples of articles, interventions, and outcomes by reclassifying them independently several weeks after the original classification. The following percent agreements were obtained for the variables under study, with their respective kappa values and probabilities (see Fleiss, 1973):

- articles by knowledge purpose: 92 percent, $\kappa = .86$, $p < .0001$
- interventions' replicability: 86 percent, $\kappa = .72$, $p < .001$
- outcomes' measurement specificity: 90 percent, $\kappa = .77$, $p < .0001$
- outcomes according to their role in the study (intermediate compared with ultimate): 95 percent, $\kappa = .77$, $p < .0001$.

Table 2.2. Numbers, Percentages, and Ranges of Research Articles by Knowledge Domain

Knowledge Domain	Number	%	Range of Articles Classified in Each Domain across 13 Journals Sampled (%)
Descriptive	314	36.0	20.0–70.0
Explanatory	423	49.0	20.0–72.0
Control-oriented	126	15.0	2.0–49.0
Total	863	100.0	

Results

The study's sample of 13 journals yielded a total of 1,849 articles, of which 863 (47 percent) met the criteria for research articles. The research articles in journals ranged from a low of 14 percent to a high of 73 percent. Six journals had more than 50 percent research articles (because our aim was to assess publications in social work, we do not report findings by specific journals).

Articles reporting research directed toward explanation were most numerous, constituting almost half (49 percent) of the total research articles. Research for descriptive knowledge was second, with 36 percent of the articles. Research for control knowledge made up 15 percent of the total number of research articles published. There was considerable variability among journals in publication of descriptive, explanatory, and control-oriented research articles. The percentage of descriptive articles across the 13 journals ranged from a low of 20 percent to a high of 70 percent; of explanatory articles from 20 percent to 72 percent; and of control-oriented research articles from 2 percent to 49 percent, consistent with their overall low rate (Table 2.2).

REPLICABILITY AND OUTCOME SPECIFICITY

The 126 control-oriented research articles investigated a total of 147 interventions in relation to outcomes. Of the 147 interventions, 65 (44 percent) met our criteria of replicability, and 82 (56 percent) did not. Replicable interventions were used in 53 of the 126 studies (42 percent), and 73 studies (58 percent) did not contain any replicable interventions.

The 126 articles investigated interventions in relation to 232 ultimate outcomes and 68 intermediate outcomes. More than half of all outcomes (57 percent) were measured with high specificity, more than a third (37 percent) were measured with medium specificity, and relatively few (6 percent) were measured with low specificity (Table 2.3). The association between specificity of measurement and outcome type was significant,

Table 2.3. Ultimate and Intermediate Outcomes by Specificity of Measurement

Measurement Specificity	Outcomes		Total
	Intermediate	Ultimate	
High	22	150	172
Medium	38	73	111
Low	8	9	17
Total	68	232	300

suggesting that ultimate outcomes, compared with intermediate outcomes, were more likely to be well specified [$\chi^2(2, N = 300) = 23.99, p < .001$].

RELATION OF REPLICABILITY OF INTERVENTION TO OUTCOME SPECIFICITY

The association between specificity of the ultimate outcomes and replicability of interventions (Table 2.4) was significant [$\chi^2(2, N = 232) = 8.36, p = .015$] but attributable to the small frequency in the low specificity condition. When low and medium specificity were joined, a two-by-two chi-square analysis was not significant [$\chi^2(1, N = 232) = .02, p = .869$], suggesting that level of specificity in measurement of ultimate outcomes was unrelated to replicability of the interventions. On the other hand, the association for intermediate outcomes was significant for a two-by-three and for a two-by-two analysis [$\chi^2(2, N = 68) = 22.02, p < .001$, and $\chi^2(1, N = 68) = 21.99, p < .001$, respectively]. Unlike ultimate outcomes, intermediate outcomes were more likely to be measured specifically in studies using replicable rather than nonreplicable interventions.

Discussion

Our review of journal publications concerned the contribution of current social work research to knowledge for guiding interventions. We focused on

Table 2.4. Specificity of Ultimate and Intermediate Outcomes Measurement by Replicability of Interventions

Intervention Replicable	Outcome						Total
	Ultimate			Intermediate			
	High Specificity	Medium Specificity	Low Specificity	High Specificity	Medium Specificity	Low Specificity	
Yes	66	37	0	16	6	1	126
No	84	36	9	6	32	7	174
Total	150	73	9	22	38	8	300

research supporting the control functions of practice—those concerned with selection and implementation of interventions—because research informing this aspect of practice traditionally has been underrepresented in social work. Our assessment of control studies was singularly concerned with those aspects of the design that we viewed as the most basic prerequisites for a profession's knowledge base—specifying the interventions and outcomes investigated in a manner that enables valid replication in research and application in practice. Accordingly, we chose not to address other features of the research, such as the populations and problems studied, sampling, control of alternative hypotheses, or theoretical bases of the interventions.

The journals sampled were expected to contain a relatively high proportion of research articles. In light of our journal selection criteria and comparisons with previous studies of journal publications, we view our journal sample as quite appropriate for the study's purpose, yet we acknowledge the possibility that the journal selection may have been influenced by our direct practice orientation. We found that reports of research were less than half (47 percent) the total articles in the journals. This number is slightly lower than the number reported by Fraser et al. (1991) and Glisson (1995) for articles published a decade before our study (between 1985 and 1988), but it is appreciably higher than the number reported by Tripodi (1984) for publications of two decades ago. It appears that the relative volume of research publications in social work has not increased during the past decade.

In evaluating the contributions of research to a profession's knowledge base, the extent to which it addresses the needs of practice is the question of primary importance. Therefore, we assessed the relative emphasis placed on research aimed at the descriptive, explanatory, and control knowledge needs of practice. We found that 36 percent of all studies aimed at descriptive knowledge, 49 percent pursued knowledge for explanation of events, and only 15 percent addressed control functions—interventions in relation to practice outcomes. Thus, fewer than one in six research studies was devoted to the central issue facing the profession—the development of effective interventions. When compared with all the articles published, only one in 14 articles (7 percent) on average reported research on intervention. This amount of control-oriented research articles is lower than the 12 percent (279 of 2,273 articles) reported by Gorey (1996). But his criteria for intervention studies were more lax—he based his definition on key words in the articles' titles or abstracts rather than on the contents of the articles. His sample also included foreign journals and non–social work publications.

Others share our concern about the relative scarcity in social work of research on intervention. McMahon, Reisch, and Patti (1991) stated that "as never before, social work needs better, more demonstrably effective intervention technologies to use with client populations that present increasingly chronic and difficult problems. Professional practitioners simply require more usable information about what works with whom, under what circumstances" (p. 5).

Schilling (1997) observed recently that although social work journals contain no shortage of articles on approaches to helping, these articles are not systematic studies designed to test the effectiveness of interventions. The Task Force on Social Work Research (1991) concluded that practitioners' needs for information about the comparative effectiveness of alternative interventions under specific conditions simply were unmet by social work researchers. And Ell (1996) expressed both surprise and concern that "there have been few controlled studies of social work interventions" (p. 585).

It is not only that social work needs more control-oriented research, but also that such research must be designed to ensure that its results can be applied by practitioners and contribute cumulatively to the profession's knowledge base. Particularly when investigating the effectiveness of complex (multicomponent) interventions, we previously proposed the following features as part of an ideal design:

· The intervention's response components (worker's actions) must be detailed in specific behavioral terms to enable reliable enactment and replication.
· The relative weight (intensity or duration) of each response component must be known and prespecified.
· The temporal order of the different response components must be indicated.
· The predicted relationship of the intervention to the attainment of specific outcomes (the practice hypothesis) must be detailed. (Rosen & Proctor, 1978)

Only one of these criteria was used in this article to assess the adequacy of intervention studies—whether the intervention's response components were described in sufficient enough detail to permit re-enactment with minimal error by practitioners and in subsequent studies. Unless this minimal requirement is met, a study's contribution to professional knowledge is questionable. Regrettably, we found that fewer than half of the studies on intervention (53 of 126) met this criterion. In other words, only 3 percent of all published articles (53 of 1,849) could inform a practitioner of how to implement reliably the intervention that was studied.

The outcomes used in the studies also were addressed. Appreciably more ultimate outcomes than intermediate outcomes were studied (232 compared with 68, respectively)—an understandable emphasis in research evaluating the effectiveness of practice. The specificity of an outcome's measurement and its role in the study were found to be associated. Ultimate outcomes were more likely than intermediate outcomes to be defined specifically, perhaps because standardized measures are more available for ultimate clinical outcomes than for intermediate, process-type outcomes. However, intermediate outcomes used in studies with replicable interventions were more likely to be well specified than intermediate outcomes in studies with nonreplicable interventions. It seems that investigators who attended well to the interventions were more likely to have measured the intermediate outcomes well, too. On the other hand, studies with nonreplicable interventions were as likely to use well-specified ultimate outcomes as were studies with replicable interventions.

Conclusion

Our survey of current social work journals revealed relatively little research on interventions, and much of that research had basic methodological flaws, detracting from its contribution to knowledge and to practice. Although research methodology is important, the paucity of research devoted to the control needs of practice is of greater and longer-range concern at present. The apparent preference of social workers for descriptive and explanatory research and the relative neglect of research on intervention undoubtedly are influenced by many factors. Understanding the factors that contribute to these preferences may assist in devising means to influence social workers' research priorities.

Many people in social work have been socialized into the researcher's role—directly by teachers and indirectly through textbooks, in the orientation and tradition of the social sciences. Such socialization may lead to the unwitting adoption of social science's emphasis on research for descriptive and explanatory purposes as a sufficient focus for research in social work (Rosen, 1996). For example, in a long-standing favorite research textbook, also used extensively in social work doctoral programs, the psychologist Fred Kerlinger (1986) states that the ultimate aim of science is the building of theory to explain and predict natural phenomena. In the same tradition, a popular research textbook for social workers (Rubin & Babbie, 1993) presents the primary purposes of social work research as being exploration, description, and explanation, omitting mention of the purpose of control.

Viewing the aims of research from an explanatory perspective also is related to the incorrect (and often implicit) assumption that the ability to explain and predict a phenomenon is tantamount to the ability to influence and change it. This assumption is implicit in Rubin and Babbie's (1993) exposition of research purposes for social workers. But it is explicit in Kerlinger (1986): "If by using a theory we are able to predict successfully, then the theory is confirmed and this is enough. . . . Since we can predict reliably, we can control because control is deducible from prediction" (p. 10). This statement erroneously equates passive and active prediction. With such a view social workers may be oblivious to the unique function of control knowledge in practice and to the need for research to address this function.

As research in social work becomes more complex and sophisticated so that it can deal with the realities of practice, it needs to become increasingly collaborative and interdisciplinary as well. A mutually beneficial collaboration requires that the participants be able to advance their own legitimate objectives as well as the common goals. The benefits to social work from interdisciplinary collaboration will be furthered materially when social work researchers keep a clear focus and work to fulfill the unique research needs and priorities of social work.

Research on the effectiveness of interventions must be a joint effort of researchers and practitioners. Whereas research that aims to describe or explain practice-relevant events can be conducted with little intrusion into the prevailing procedures of practice, research on intervention mandates such intrusion. Thus, collaboration in research on intervention is dependent not only on the ingenuity of the researcher in adapting research requirements to the realities of practice, but also on the willingness of practitioners to accommodate such research in the practice environment. We believe that the likelihood of successful researcher–practitioner collaboration will be enhanced greatly if researchers and practitioners share their understandings of the various knowledge needs of practice, distinguish between passive and active prediction tasks, and appreciate some of the basic design requirements for testing control knowledge and studying the effectiveness of interventions.

References

Beck, A. T., Ward, C. H., Mendelson, M., Mock, J., & Erbaugh, J. (1961). An inventory for measuring depression. *Archives of General Psychiatry, 12,* 63–70.

Chambless, D. L., & Hollon, S. D. (1998). Defining empirically supported therapies. *Journal of Clinical and Consulting Psychology, 66,* 7–18.

Ell, K. (1996). Social work and health care practice and policy: A psychosocial research agenda. *Social Work, 41,* 583–592.

Fleiss, J. L. (1973). *Statistical methods for rates and proportions.* New York: John Wiley & Sons.

Fraser, M., Taylor, M. E., Jackson, R., & O'Jack, J. (1991). Social work and science: Many ways of knowing? *Social Work Research & Abstracts, 27*(4), 5–15.

Glisson, C. (1995). The state of art of social work research: Implications for mental health. *Research on Social Work Practice, 5,* 205–222.

Gorey, K. M. (1996). Effectiveness of social work intervention research: Internal versus external evaluators. *Social Work Research, 20,* 119–128.

Greenwood, E. (1957). Social work research—A decade of reappraisal. *Social Service Review, 31,* 311–321.

Kadushin, A. (1959). The knowledge base of social work. In A. J. Kahn (Ed.), *Issues in American social work* (pp. 39–79). New York: Columbia University Press.

Kane, R. A. (1982). Lessons for social work from the medical model: A viewpoint for practice. *Social Work, 27,* 315–321.

Kerlinger, F. L. (1986). *Foundations of behavioral research* (3rd ed.). New York: Harcourt Brace Jovanovich.

Klein, W. C., & Bloom, M. (1994). Social work as applied social science: A historical analysis. *Social Work, 39,* 421–431.

Lindsey, D., & Kirk, S. A. (1992). The role of social work journals in the development of a knowledge base for the profession. *Social Service Review, 66,* 295–310.

McMahon, M. O., Reisch, M., & Patti, R. J. (1991). *Scholarship in social work: Integration of research, teaching, & service.* Washington, DC: National Association of Deans and Directors of Schools of Social Work.

Mutschler, E., & Rosen, A. (1979). Evaluation of treatment outcomes by client and social worker. *Social Welfare Forum, 106,* 156–165.

Nelsen, J. (1984). Intermediate treatment goals as variables in single-case research. *Social Work Research & Abstracts, 20*(3), 3–10.

Proctor, E. K., & Rosen, A. (1983). Problem formulation and its relation to treatment planning. *Social Work Research & Abstracts, 19*(3), 22–28.

Rosen, A. (1978). Issues in educating for the knowledge-building research doctorate. *Social Service Review, 52,* 437–448.

Rosen, A. (1993). Systematic planned practice. *Social Service Review, 67,* 84–100.

Rosen, A. (1996). The scientific practitioner revisited: Some obstacles and prerequisites for fuller implementation in practice. *Social Work Research, 20,* 105–111.

Rosen, A., & Proctor, E. K. (1978). Specifying the treatment process: The basis for effectiveness research. *Journal of Social Service Research, 2,* 25–43.

Rosen A., & Proctor, E. K. (1981). Distinctions between treatment outcomes and their implications for treatment evaluation. *Journal of Consulting and Clinical Psychology, 49,* 418–425.

Rosen, A., Proctor, E. K., & Livne, S. (1985). Planning and direct practice. *Social Service Review, 59,* 161–167.

Rosen, A., Proctor, E. K., Morrow-Howell, N., & Staudt, M. (1995). Rationale for practice decisions: Variations in knowledge use by decision task and social work service. *Research on Social Work Practice, 5,* 501–523.

Rubin, A., & Babbie, E. (1993). *Research methods for social work* (2nd ed.). Pacific Grove, CA: Brooks/Cole.

Schilling, R. F. (1997). Developing intervention research programs in social work. *Social Work Research, 21,* 173–180.

Task Force on Social Work Research. (1991). *Building social work knowledge for effective services and policies: A plan for research development.* Washington, DC: NASW Press.

Tolman, R. M., & Molidor, C. E. (1994). A decade of social group work research: Trends in methodology, theory, and program development. *Research on Social Work Practice, 4,* 142–159.

Tripodi, T. (1984). Trends in research publication: A study of social work journals from 1956 to 1980. *Social Work, 29,* 353–359.

Yeaton, W. H., & Sechrest, L. (1981). Critical dimensions in the choice and maintenance of successful treatments: Trends, integrity, and effectiveness. *Journal of Consulting and Clinical Psychology, 49,* 156–167.

CHAPTER 3

Paradigmatic Influences in Practice Research: A Critical Assessment

Mansoor A. F. Kazi

This chapter reviews the main contemporary trends in practice research in England. The review is based on some of the key publications on evaluation of social work practice that have emerged between 1995 and 1997 and on the recent experience of the Centre for Evaluation Studies at the University of Huddersfield. The chapter begins with the complexities of effectiveness in social work, then proceeds to critically analyze the contributions and limitations of each of the main research paradigms in apprehending the realities of social work practice and its effectiveness. These perspectives are identified as empirical practice, pragmatism, critical theory, and scientific realism—the latter being a new addition to the family. The recent growth in the practice research enterprise in England is in direct response to the radical changes that have taken place in the settings and contexts in which practice operates.

The pressures on social work practice to demonstrate its effectiveness have continued to grow in the last two decades in England. Legal and societal changes have shifted the context of the profession: the value of social work is no longer taken for granted and its worth now has to be demonstrated (Parton, 1994). The Children Act (1989) and the Community Care Act (1990) both include requirements for needs-led assessments, planning, and progress reviews. The purchaser-provider split, the growth of the voluntary and private sectors alongside the public sector, and the introduction of competition for contracts also have made monitoring and evaluation more central to social work practice. Resources are finite, yet social needs are complex and in a state of flux. Effectiveness research offers one way to make social programs accountable and to enable politicians, agencies, and practitioners to make hard choices in the allocation of scarce resources.

Apart from accountability and the need to demonstrate the worth of social work practice, practice research serves another purpose—the need to develop and improve the content of social work practice so that it can better meet the needs of its clients and the wider society. Therefore, effectiveness practice research has two main purposes—providing evidence of the worth of social work practice, and striving to improve that practice as it responds to changing needs and contexts. Whether emphasis is placed on one or the other or both of these purposes depends on the paradigmatic influences inherent in the effectiveness researcher's activities.

Complexities of Social Work Practice

Social work practice has been defined as "an activity which enables individuals, families, and groups to identify personal, social, and environmental difficulties adversely affecting them. Social work enables them to manage these difficulties through supportive, rehabilitative, protective or corrective action" (Central Council for Education and Training in Social Work, 1989, p. 8).

Social work practice takes place in an open system, usually in a holistic relationship with the social work client; it cannot, therefore, operate without taking into account the person's environment or context. Social work interventions usually take place at the interface of the individual and society, where multiple factors and influences are continuously at work. In such circumstances the best result a scientific researcher can strive for is an explanation that approximates the realities of practice, and the best achievable result is probabilistic knowledge.

Figure 3.1 attempts to illustrate the complexities of social work practice. Effectiveness questions may include ethics and the value-base, processes (including the process of assessment, the content of intervention, and the social work theory on which the practice strategy is based), and the outcomes of social work practice, as a first dimension. These factors may need to be addressed from the perspectives of service users, social workers, managers, other professionals, and significant others relevant to the practice—who together constitute the second dimension. Both of these dimensions are underpinned by the context in which social work takes place, including the influences from the underlying mechanisms, structures, and systems. Figure 3.1 is, of course, a very crude attempt to illustrate these complexities. Because the factors within each dimension are in a continuous state of flux, they cannot be characterized as blocks with distinct boundaries.

The complexities of practice are such that outcome data alone may not provide a relevant perspective on whether the outcomes achieved actually were desirable given the clients' circumstances within the context of

Figure 3.1.

Dimensions of Practice

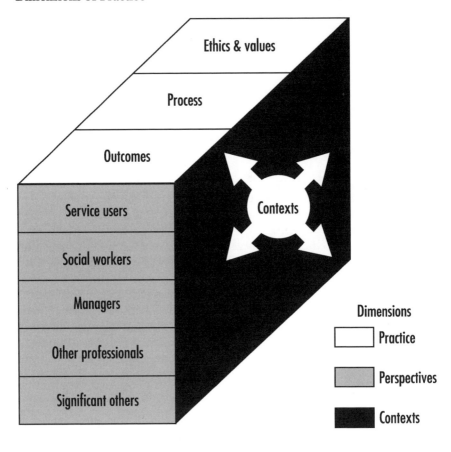

practice. In order to develop more effective practice, it helps to know not only the extent to which client objectives were achieved, but also which process was effective and under what circumstances. The context of practice is fluid and inherently unpredictable; at the same time, failure to address context renders any explanation at best incomplete. Even if scrutiny of the data finds that the desirable outcomes were achieved with most service users—and even if a causal link between process and outcome can be established—if the effectiveness strategy addresses the practice and perspective dimensions superficially, without digging deeper into contexts, such an explanation will be incomplete. It will not address why the program was successful with some clients and not with others. Future successes cannot be guaranteed.

The researcher can either gather superficial data or attempt to dig deeper into the contexts. The dimensions of practice targeted by the researcher, and the extent to which the complexities are addressed, depend on (a) the paradigmatic perspective of the researcher, and (b) the extent to which that particular perspective enables the researcher to address these complexities.

Effectiveness research—or any other type of research—cannot be driven by the methodology to the exclusion of paradigmatic influences. The ontology and epistemology of the researcher profoundly affect what is researched and how, including the researcher's choice of effectiveness questions. Whether effectiveness of social work practice is seen in a holistic way, whether emphasis is placed on processes or outcomes (or on user or other perspectives), even decisions regarding the feasibility of particular methodologies to address the selected questions—these also are subject to paradigmatic influences. Even if the researcher adopts an outcome-oriented perspective (such as empirical practice) that does not include value issues in its repertoire (Thyer, 1993), the researcher's own value-base is part of the paradigmatic influence, and therefore the research process itself is not value free.

A Review of Contemporary Research Perspectives

Four main perspectives influence social work practice research in England at the present time:

1. empirical practice (for example, Kazi & Wilson, 1996; Macdonald, 1996)
2. pragmatism or methodological pluralism (for example, Cheetham et al., 1992; Fuller, 1996; Fuller & Petch, 1995; Kazi, 1998)
3. critical theory (for example, Everitt & Hardiker, 1996; Shaw, 1996, 1998)
4. scientific realism (Pawson & Tilley, 1997a, 1997b).

This classification resembles that in Trinder (1996) except for scientific realism, which emerged only in the last year in England although it had already developed in the United States (see Anastas & MacDonald, 1994). Any attempt at such a classification can only be a crude attempt, as the boundaries tend to be indistinct and these perspectives often overlap. For example, what is here called *scientific realism* is placed by others in the same category as empirical practice under the term *postpositivism* (Fraser et al., 1991). A further reason why these boundaries are not so clear cut is that, unlike the great epistemological debate in the United States, in the main these four perspectives share the same ontology. As for which perspective dominates practice, Trinder (1996) notes that most Department of Health-funded research is in fact pragmatist, based on nonexperimental quantitative methodologies including surveys—a view corroborated by American reviews of the products of social work research (Fraser et al., 1991).

The contemporary paradigms in social work research reflect the debates in the philosophies of social science. The basis for these controversies lies in the demise of foundationism, on which the earlier version of positivism was based. In the earlier part of the 20th century, the positivist paradigm was dominant, along with the positions that positive knowledge was based on causal laws of phenomena derived from observation. Positivism held that the world could be observed as it was through the senses. Propositions that could not be tested or verified—in other words, those beyond sensory experience—were deemed to be meaningless. However, Karl Popper, Kuhn, and others challenged the view that knowledge could be based on facts as absolute truths. Scientific knowledge could not achieve absolute certainty in terms of facts, as observation was both theory-laden and value-laden. At best, scientific knowledge was probabilistic knowledge—what is known today is an approximation of truth, and such approximations change and develop as progress is made. There is no certain way to compare a theory to theory-neutral reality, and therefore, the problem of science or knowledge cannot finally be resolved (Manicas, 1987). The world cannot be known as it is, because it is mediated by socially and historically constituted practices. Therefore, choices between competing theories (for example, theories of social support) depend on the mixture of objective and subjective factors of individual and shared criteria among those making the selections. In other words, no research process can be perfect—there are always limitations, and the findings from research can be true only until further notice.

A number of antipositivist paradigms emerged from this realization, holding different ontological and epistemological positions—and these are also reflected in the contemporary publications in British social work research. If the philosophy of science holds that truth and certainty are not attainable, then at the level of ontology (theories about the nature of being), one must make choices. One can take the position that a reality exists out there in the world and that one can use the reflection of this reality (no matter how imperfect) as a standard toward which to strive. Or one can take the philosophy of uncertainty to its ultimate conclusion, that there is no reality that can be used as a standard, and that therefore many truths exist which are all equally true even if they contradict one another. The first position is known as realism; the second position is that of some (but not all) interpretivist approaches, such as constructivism or postmodernity. Constructivism holds that realities exist in the form of multiple mental constructs (Guba, 1990).

In England such relativist perspectives tend to be underrepresented in practice research. In the recent books on practice research reviewed in this chapter, only one—Everitt and Hardiker (1996)—attempts to advocate postmodernist relativism, which holds that there is no single truth or single approximation of truth, and that all conflicting perspectives are potentially true. However, as we shall see, the perspective expressed by Everitt and

Hardiker is ontologically confused, as they attempt to combine relativism with a mainly critical theorist perspective, which holds that a single truth indeed exists.

EMPIRICAL PRACTICE MOVEMENT

Empirical practice tends to be associated with positivism. However, it is impossible to describe positivism in the sense of a single paradigm or to sufficiently capture its essence in a single description to satisfy even those researchers who admit to following positivism. Outhwaite (1987) notes at least twelve varieties of positivism. Therefore any single description of positivism as a paradigm will fail to do full justice to all the variants. A further complication in social work effectiveness research is that, in the main, people tend to get on with the job of developing and applying positivist methodologies in practice without necessarily standing back and describing the exact variant (or variants) of positivism that influences them most. In social work circles, positivism is identified with methodology rather than with a perspective. Researchers who promote, say, randomized controlled trials or single-case designs, or those who want to apply outcome measures to effectiveness in order to provide evidence for testing social work interventions, tend to be associated with a single entity called positivism.

A drawback of the failure to identify the particular ontology or epistemology of positivist researchers is that, in the great epistemological debate, they all tend to be tarred with the same brush. And at times they may be tarred together with the most extreme version of positivism that an antipositivist can find. An example from the American epistemological debate is Tyson's (1992) assertion that all proponents of empirical practice in social work assume that observation is theory free. An assumption is made that empirical practice in social work is associated with foundationist positivism, which believes in the certainty of objective knowledge as a true reflection of reality, or in the certainty of causal links between phenomena. The British social work version of the debate tends to be less extreme—for example, Shaw (1996) draws a line between the various forms of positivism that he criticizes (largely from the standpoint of critical theory) and Popperian antideterministic objectivity, and also cautions social workers against confining neopositivism or Popper to the dustbin. Also, from a critical theoretical standpoint (as well as relativist postmodernity), Everitt and Hardiker (1996) criticize empirical practice but accept that randomized controlled trials may be useful in some circumstances.

In practice research in England, two main movements appear to be associated with empirical practice or evidence-based perspective. One movement promotes single-case evaluation procedures that could be used by practitioners to ascertain the effects of their practice through the measurement of client outcomes. This author's work to promote the use of single-case evaluation by social work practitioners in a variety of settings has been reported elsewhere (Kazi 1996, 1997). The second movement promotes the use of randomized controlled trials (RCTs) that can establish causal links between the social work programs and their effects with greater confidence. This trend is seen in the recent publications of the biggest children's charity in Britain, Barnardos (Macdonald, 1996; Oakley, 1996).

THE CONTRIBUTION OF EMPIRICAL PRACTICE

At first, the empirical practice approach dominated most effectiveness strategies. This approach was the first to recognize the need for providing evidence of effectiveness and to develop effectiveness strategies (for example, by drawing a distinction between the intervention and its effects). Also, the focus on outcomes with this approach lends itself to an emphasis on effectiveness in the (albeit narrow) sense of social work practice causing a desired effect.

The antipositivist approaches tended to be preoccupied with describing or exploring questions of process and context, which were felt to be more important than providing evidence of effectiveness. Earlier stages of the epistemological debate within social work research circles centered around whether it was possible or even desirable, given the complexities of social work, to address effectiveness questions (Jordan, 1978; Sheldon, 1978). Although the earlier questions have by no means been resolved, to the extent that critics of empirical practice are now attempting to develop alternative effectiveness strategies the debate has shifted to how questions of effectiveness could be addressed (Everitt & Hardiker, 1996; Shaw, 1996).

An important contribution of empirical practice is the drawing of a distinction between the social work programs and their effects. Going back to Figure 3.1, empirical practice enables a distinction to be made between the processes and the outcomes of social work, in the realm of practice (the top or surface of the box). Empirical practice also attempts to link the process and outcomes in ways that enable at least some evidence of progress by which the effects of the process can be judged. At most it enables a causal link to be made between the process and the outcome to strengthen such judgments. Empiricists believe that scientific procedures such as the hypothetico-deductive approach can be applied to social work practice, and that knowledge is based on observable phenomena that can provide the evidence of outcomes. For example, Martin and Kettner (1996, p. 3) note that "performance measurement incorporates a focus on outcomes (in other words, the results, impacts, and accomplishments) of human service programs" (see also Bryman, 1988; Thyer, 1993). Hypotheses to be tested may be formulated as causal connections between variables or simply as statements that the introduction of an independent variable (for example, the intervention) would lead to changes in the dependent variable (for example, client objectives). Hypotheses of either formulation are then empirically tested in the form of outcome measures that provide evidence.

LIMITATIONS OF EMPIRICAL PRACTICE

Empirical practice researchers acknowledge the limitations of this approach. For example, in the application of the gold standard of RCTs, technical limitations may interfere. No-treatment control groups or random allocation to groups may not be possible, for example, and the trials may be too expensive. Still, it is argued, RCTs potentially offer something other study methods cannot—"maximum security in results" (Macdonald, 1996, p. 23).

At the lower end of the hierarchy of positivist methods, Kazi, Mantysaari, and Rostila (1997) also acknowledge the limitations of single-case designs. Specifically, they acknowledge the following limiting characteristics:

· This methodology is a verification procedure and cannot determine what the intervention itself should be.
· This methodology cannot, because of the requirement for repeated measurement, be applied to social work that involves a single contact with the client.
· This methodology cannot represent the full perspective of any party, the desirability of the intervention, or the context of practice.
· This methodology cannot assess issues of ethics and values.
· This methodology is pre-experimental and therefore cannot with confidence establish a causal link as the RCTs can.

More generally, a major limitation of empirical practice is that its focus on effects virtually excludes consideration of the content of the intervention being tested. "The weakness of the hypothetico-deductive system, in so far as it might profess to offer a complete account of the scientific process, lies in its disclaiming any power to explain how hypotheses come into being" (Medawar, 1982, p. 135).

Even if RCTs are used, this central limitation remains. Oakley (1996) provides examples of RCTs that, while providing a robust examination of the effects of a social program, also fail to address the content of the program itself. For instance, RCTs were used to test the effectiveness of social support for pregnant women. Oakley provides an extensive analysis of the types of outcomes and the characteristics of the random groups, but there is extremely little information about the nature of the social support program itself, nor is there any evidence of a dynamic approach to the development of the nature of social support. This limitation is not just a question of methodology that can be addressed in future applications. While some improvements could be made in future applications, the central issue here is one of the paradigm—the ontology and epistemology of the researcher using the methodologies. The limitation of virtually ignoring content is at the heart of the hypothetico-deductive paradigm.

Empirical practice tends to operate as if there were no canons for reasoning by which rational methods of arriving at theories and better hypotheses could be controlled. To concentrate on test results—or performance outcomes—may inform this process, but it is one-sided in the sense that it does not provide the means of developing such theories. Instead, it virtually ignores the content of what it tests empirically. For example, Macdonald (1996) provides an example of ice therapy—a view put to her by some social workers that a particular type of ice therapy was a beneficial intervention for particular children. Macdonald uses this example to imply that, without evidence-based practice, anything of this sort goes. However, the use of RCTs in themselves will not prevent it. On the contrary, because it is methodology- and test-driven to the extent that content is virtually ignored, there is also a danger that it could corroborate the literal effectiveness of such interventions without due regard to the moral, value-laden, theoretical, and contextual issues that are central to social work practice. Therefore, on the basis of this epistemological and ontological limitation, it could be argued that empirical practice alone does not provide a complete account of science as it is applied to the effectiveness of social work practice. In other words, to research the content of an intervention (and the contexts underpinning practice) in addition to its effects, empirical practice approaches need to be combined with others, to provide a more complete explanation of the realities of social work practice.

A second limitation arises from attempts to control for intervening variables rather than provide an explanation of the actual structures, mechanisms, and systems and the complex interrelationships that exist in the open system. The models that are applied are not models that could explain the reality of the open system—that is, the real entities that exist. The isolation of two variables and the establishment of a causal link between them cannot predict reality, as it does not explain the complexities of the open system. Empirical practice may establish links between the intervention and its effects, but it does not explain why a particular effect arose. For example, even if an intervention is found to be effective with the majority of clients, typically no explanation exists as to why it was not effective with others. "Confirmation principle fails to include explanation—scientific method is interested not only in correlations that can be discovered, but also explanations as to why" (Harre, 1984, p. 47). The causal link at the surface, without explanation of the underlying mechanisms, contexts, and structures, is insufficient for evidence-based practice of the kind advocated by Myers and Thyer (1997) or by Macdonald (1996). This is because a superficial causal link does not provide an explanation based on real entities and mechanisms; at best it is descriptive and does not take contexts into account—contexts that are inherently unpredictable.

An intervention that is effective in one context may not be so in another context, even if it could be described in such a way that it could be replicated. Hence, in Oakley's example of social support for pregnant women, changes may occur in the type of social support, as it cannot be kept static, least of all when its content is not addressed. Or the approach adopted in a particular context for a particular client group may not work in another context or for another client group. We do not know what it is that explains the causal relationship that has been demonstrated—all we know is that the study does demonstrate a causal relationship. A generative causal link is required for the kind of evidence-base that demonstrates one intervention theory as being more effective than another. It is insufficient to know that a link was established; we also need to know what generative mechanism caused the intervention to be effective. In other words, why is an intervention effective or not effective, and in what circumstances? The establishment of a causal link that is successive rather than generative is, by itself, not sufficient as hard evidence to discard theories that do not work. If all that can be proven is that a program worked, this proof could be obtained merely by systematically tracking clients' progress.

This discussion is based on realist interpretations of the contribution and limitations of empirical practice—its main contributions to practice are recognized and valued. The criticisms made here relate to two things:

1. Neopositivist forms of reasoning are unsatisfactory only if they are put forward as exclusive and complete accounts of the scientific method.
2. The limitations of neopositivist forms of reasoning apply to social work effectiveness in that empirical practice approaches by themselves cannot address the full complexities (or explain the generative mechanisms and other real entities) that enable or disable social work programs to be effective.

These arguments do not imply that methodologies originating from positivism are inapplicable and therefore should be discarded, or that positivism should be treated as a swear word in social work circles. On the contrary, while empirical practice offers, at best, a partial account of reality, so do other paradigms such as those based on critical theory. The point is that, because the contribution made is partial rather than holistic, the empirical practice approaches are limited in addressing the full complexities of social work practice.

Pragmatism or Methodological Pluralism

Fuller (1996, p. 59) outlines three basic elements of the methodological-pluralist or pragmatic approach:

1. Suspension of unresolvable philosophical conundra in the interests of getting on with the job.

2. The making of contextual judgments about the trade-off between what
   might be desirable, by way of research design, and what is feasible. Such
   judgments may involve what may seem to some like a dangerously
   impure regard for credibility of certain research methods with intended
   audiences.
3. Abandonment of the search for the evaluator's magic wand that would
   turn all to the gold of irrefutable scientific proof.

Central to the pragmatist position is the desire to "get on with the job" of
effectiveness research. Fuller's position appears to be antiphilosophical,
considering the epistemological debates to be a waste of time as the issues
debated around the comparison of theory with theory-neutral reality
cannot be resolved. This author, too, has reflected the same "getting on
with the job" trend (Kazi, 1997). These positions have led to a charge that
pragmatism is essentially an anti-intellectual trend in social work research,
and that it is an "unashamedly empirical approach to research, steering a
course between the scientific empiricism of the positivist project and the
messier politicized approach to research of participative/critical researchers" (Trinder, 1996). Pragmatism also has been attacked as "anything goes"
(Macdonald, 1996). In fact, the advent of the pragmatic approach to
mixing methods is a consequence of the epistemological debate, in the
sense that this debate has helped to (a) recognize the limitations of the
methods associated with each paradigm, and (b) enable the realization that
qualitative methods are acceptable and can be combined with quantitative
methods to present a more comprehensive approximation of reality. Ontologically, pragmatists draw the line at relativism; therefore—at least at the
level of ontology—this approach is not "anything goes."

The mixing of methods in effectiveness studies (for example, as reported
in Kazi, 1997, 1998, where single-case evaluation was combined with other
methods in the evaluation of adult rehabilitation programs) was influenced
by the pragmatic approach advocated by colleagues at the University of
Stirling in Scotland. Cheetham and others (1992) describe this approach as
"eclectic, not wedded to a single alliance," and explain that because of the
"diversity, occasional elusiveness and the generally shifting sands of social
policy in action," adherence to a single approach "would risk leaving much
social work activity unresearchable" (p. 20).

Feasibility is an important factor in the selection of methods. One should
begin with the evaluation questions and then select a method (or a
combination of methods) that can be applied appropriately to address the
relevant questions. Typical methods are secondary analyses (study of records), monitoring devices (some measures), questionnaires, interviews,
scales and schedules, observation, and diaries with a largely quantitative
base (but with some efforts at gaining qualitative insights).

The empirical practice distinction between process and outcomes is
accepted, but various ways exist for addressing the connection between

them. "Indeed, it can be forcibly argued that a sophisticated understanding of social work, and indeed all the human services, should now be informed by these two rather different kinds of knowledge—in jargon, about outcomes and processes—and seek to connect them" (Cheetham, 1998, pp. 9–10). Within this perspective, for example, single-case evaluation or RCTs would not be seen as an empirical revolution, but as one of a range of equally valid methods available to evaluate social work practice. The limitations of each methodology would be recognized, and other methods would be used to address the questions that any one methodology was unable to address.

For example, one of the main weaknesses of the single-case evaluation studies (Kazi & Wilson, 1996) was their focus on measures of effectiveness rather than on the actual content of the social work programs. In the later adult rehabilitation studies (Kazi, 1998), content was an important question for inquiry, and qualitative methodologies (for example, focus groups influenced by critical theory) were used to explore the nature of the social programs—the actual services provided, and the values and theories underpinning them. The richness of the data obtained through the use of both positivist and naturalistic approaches enabled the author to draw more informed inferences regarding the project's effectiveness.

ADVANTAGES AND LIMITATIONS OF PRAGMATISM

Going back to Figure 3.1, through combining various approaches, the pragmatist approach takes on board the advantages of empirical practice and attempts to compensate for its limitations through triangulation. A pragmatist approach defines effectiveness in the empirical practice sense of drawing a distinction between the social work intervention and its effects, and effects are empirically tested using both quantitative and qualitative methodologies. At the same time, the content is analyzed with greater insight. In this way, methodological-pragmatism can dig deeper into the complexities of social work practice. More objective outcome data are combined with more subjective perspectives of all the parties concerned, and the context is also taken into account to some extent if desired. Therefore, as shown in Figure 3.1, the pragmatic approach of realist methodological pluralism not only can establish connections between process and outcomes of practice, but also between the ethics, values, and perceptions of all the parties involved. In addition, methodological pluralism digs into the context a little deeper than does the empirical practice approach.

By concentrating on the needs of stakeholders or on practice needs, methodological-pragmatism may fail to capture the effectiveness of a social work program in a holistic way. This limitation can occur particularly if the researcher tends to become essentially driven by the methodology or if the researcher considers feasibility to be the main criterion. In terms of its explanatory powers, methodological-pragmatism may concentrate on the expressed needs of the participants in negotiating questions of inquiry, and fail to capture the main features of the mechanisms which influence the effectiveness of programs in an open system. These pitfalls will ensure that although the explanation of reality may be improved when compared with empirical practice, the effectiveness of practice will be apprehended at best only partially. Furthermore, like empiricist researchers, pragmatic researchers tend to make judgments about past practice rather than developing future practice.

CRITICAL THEORIST PERSPECTIVE

The critical theorist paradigm of research is advocated in British social work by Shaw (1996) and Everitt and Hardiker (1996). It is politically oriented inquiry that includes movements aimed at the emancipation of oppressed people, including feminist, neo-Marxist, and other forms of participatory inquiry. "Evaluating in practice . . . is not about reflective rigour in empowering but concerns a practice which is legitimated only through the test of whether it empowers and emancipates. . . . Effectiveness is truth" (Shaw, 1996, p. 110). The task of the inquiry is to raise people (mainly service users, and to some extent also practitioners—but, it is implied, not managers) from the various forms of false consciousness they have due to their oppressions to a level of true consciousness that helps to emancipate oppressed people and enables them to transform their situations. The ontology is therefore by definition critical realist ("true" consciousness), coupled with a subjectivist epistemology which relates the inquiry's activities to the values of the researcher (Guba, 1990).

Methodologically, the critical theorists take a dialogic approach that aims to rally participants and raise their consciousness of reality in order to achieve desired changes. This dialogic process helps achieve greater self-knowledge and self-reflection in order to transform people toward greater autonomy and responsibility, hence linking both theory and practice. Understanding comes by change and change comes by understanding. The methodologies incorporate both empirical analyses and historical hermeneutics, but hard data are not considered to be any better than soft data. Surveys tend not to be used, as they do not reflect the full intents and purposes of people; therefore, the critical theorist's preference is for qualitative approaches that enable the researcher to dig deeper into the underlying values, meanings, and interpretations of the participants (Popkewitz, 1990). The ontology also is realist and not relativist in the sense that issues of methodology are in part related to a historical context, concerning power and control in society. The scientific process therefore interacts with the realities of the historical conditions in which it works. The process of scientific enquiry is not technical or procedural but instead embedded in values, ethics, morality, and politics. Critical theorists can combine this epistemology with others—there are two examples of this from contemporary research circles in England.

The first example (Shaw, 1996, pp. 115–116) combines critical theory with Popperian falsifiability (and other influences), suggesting the following approach to evaluation of practice:

- participatory evaluation with service users
- reflection on tacit knowing-in-practice
- description of practice in ways that render access to its strengths and weaknesses feasible
- mutual reflexivity of both practitioner and service user
- legitimation through falsifying and grounded plausibility.

Shaw retains a critical realist approach in falsifiability and grounded plausibility, and draws the line at relativism; therefore, although he is epistemologically pluralist (for example, in combining critical theory with Popperian falsifiability) and to some extent methodologically pluralist, his paradigmatic influences are based in a critical realist ontology.

The second example is that of Everitt and Hardiker (1996). On the basis of critical theory, they suggest that effectiveness research should enable a dialogue between users and the organization as well as between social workers and the organization. The purpose of such a dialogue would be to enhance both users' and social workers' feelings of being valued and to strive for high standards of good practice. These standards should include a strong emphasis on issues of power, powerlessness, race, gender, disability and social class. The purpose of effectiveness research is to make judgments about value and effect change in the direction of the "good." Critical theory helps in locating people's perceptions within the social, political, and economic contexts, particularly in relation to structural oppression and discrimination.

However, unlike Shaw, these authors attempt to steer a middle course between rational-technical and interpretivist approaches, and draw on relativist postmodern theories of knowledge. For example, one influence (Layder, 1993) sees no distinction between objectivity and subjectivity, arguing that micro and macro phenomena are inextricably bound together through the medium of social activity and are discovered through discourses. Another influence is Parton's (1994) postmodern analysis of changes in social work: "One consequence of the undermining of universal science, knowledge, and truth, is that all views, interests, and arguments are potentially valid—it relocates politics as central to everyday life" (p. 28). Everitt and Hardiker (1996) take these influences to a relativist conclusion:

> There is not one truth to be revealed but many truths and perspectives articulated, suppressed, negotiated, compromised through discourses, through processes of power

and powerlessness. Such an epistemological position, rather than claiming the truth of
the knowledge generated, allows for, indeed makes necessary, the need for moral
decision-making and judgement-making. (p. 107)

However, based on critical theory, they also present a different ontology,
one of approximation to one thing called truth (or critical realism). "Those
involved in evaluation are simultaneously seekers after truth while realising
that truth is an illusion and something to which they can only ever
approximate" (Everitt & Hardiker, 1996, p. 188).

Based on an eclectic ontology incorporating both realism and relativism,
the authors' epistemology is, on the one hand, subjectivist and relativist
where findings are based on dialogic interaction between the researcher
and the people involved in practice, with all constructs considered as
potential truths. On the other hand, it retains a modified objectivity—a
truth that can be approximated, even though what is approximated may be
an illusion. As a result, Everitt and Hardiker are inconsistent in their
effectiveness research practice. On the one hand, they recognize the many
truths in social work practice, and bring all parties together in a reflexive
dialogue; on the other, based in critical theory, they strive for an approximation of truth, or to move the dialogue from false consciousness toward true
consciousness. The researcher is in a difficult position to do both things—he
or she will not be able to follow through with either of these goals if both are
attempted at the same time. The conflict between these two positions arises
from Everitt and Hardiker's ontological pluralism, which renders the
combination of the two untenable in practice. The upshot of this dilemma
is that, while methodological pluralism is possible and even desirable in
many circumstances, ontological pluralism is fraught with difficulties.

CONTRIBUTIONS AND LIMITATIONS OF CRITICAL THEORY

Critical theorists emphasize the raising of consciousness and the emancipation of oppressed client groups that receive social work services. To the
extent that social work practice can raise consciousness or lead to emancipation, then social work is judged as good. In this context, effectiveness is
truth, and it is arrived at through focus groups, life history work, and a mix
of methods that do not exclude quantitative measures but prefer qualitative
approaches. As far as evidence-based practice is concerned, the emphasis is
placed on the perspectives and insights of the participants. Effectiveness
research contributes to this process of striving for emancipation and true
consciousness and enables judgments to be made as to whether the practice
is good. In this way, critical theory goes farther than empirical practice in
addressing the content of practice, the ethics and values, the multiple
perspectives, and to some extent the contexts as well.

Critical theorist researchers not only enjoy the advantages of the realist
methodological–pragmatic approach but also provide an additional empha-

sis on the perceptions of users and practitioners. They emphasize ethics, values, and moral issues, and attempt to make such issues part of the process and outcome of social work practice. When combined with methodological pragmatism generally (but steering clear of Everitt & Hardiker's ontological pluralism), critical theory can add a richer dimension to effectiveness research, as this author found in an evaluation of a mental health advocacy service. Standardized outcome measures from Fischer and Corcoran (1994) were combined with semistructured surveys and focus groups based on a critical theorist standpoint, providing a richer account of the process of advocacy, its effects, and the perceptions of the participants; at the same time, the process of research itself contributed to the raising of consciousness of the mental health service users.

A limitation of critical theory is that it tends to concentrate on the needs of stakeholders and their perceptions, and therefore fails to capture the effectiveness of a social work program in a holistic way. Critical theorists tend to be suspicious of attempts to measure effects of services. This tendency in part explains Shaw's (1998) heavily critical stance toward single-case evaluation even in situations where this methodology is no more than a systematic tracking of client outcomes. This one-sidedness means that critical theorist researchers will not begin with a holistic perspective, thereby failing to capture all the dimensions of social work practice as illustrated in Figure 3.1.

THE SCIENTIFIC REALIST PERSPECTIVE

A new perspective, called *scientific realism*, includes all other perspectives that share the same ontology. In other words, scientific realism excludes only foundationist positivism (which holds that reality can be apprehended as it is) and relativism (which holds that, as there is no certain truth, differing perceptions in the minds of people are all true—for example, constructivism and postmodernism).

This perspective is also known by other terms, including *transcendental realism, referential realism, fallibilistic realism, postpositivism,* or generally as a realist view of science (Fraser et al., 1991; Phillips, 1990). The term *fallibilistic realism* was first suggested by Donald Campbell in a personal communication (Manicas & Secord, 1983) and is also used by Anastas and MacDonald (1994). It is based on the work of Michael Scriven, Roy Bhaskar, and notably, the philosopher Rom Harre. This epistemological model has its basis in realism. As such, it seeks to incorporate the critiques of logical positivism without abandoning the concept of a knowable reality. Ontologically, positivist or neopositivist approaches emphasize hypothetical entities rather than real ones, seeking to generalize laws or operations established in laboratory conditions into the real world. In contrast, the realist theory of science "allows scientists to believe that they are grappling with entities that, although often not observable directly, are real enough. . . . It would seem that once they understand it, scientists would happily adopt a realist theory of science" (Manicas & Secord, 1983, p. 412).

The ontology of scientific realism is critical realist—reality exists external to the observer, and although it cannot be apprehended as it is (for the observer's theoretical orientation acts as a filter), one can strive for an approximation of this reality. As scientific knowledge develops, what appears to be an approximation of reality today may change (hence the term *fallibilistic*). In this sense, scientific realism shares the same critical realism as most of empirical practice, pragmatism, and critical theory perspectives in social work research. However, it goes farther than all of these others in recognizing that the world is an open system consisting of a constellation of structures, mechanisms and contexts.

Scientific realism "regards the objects of knowledge as the structures and mechanisms that generate phenomena; and the knowledge is produced in the social activities of science. These objects are neither phenomena (empiricism) nor human constructs imposed on the phenomena (idealism) but real structures which endure independently of our knowledge, our experience, and the conditions which allow us access to them" (Bhaskar, 1978, p. 24). Phenomena that are studied in the real world are studied in a fluid context (that is, in an open system). The activities of persons in society may be seen as a set of interacting, interwoven structures at different levels. Realism refers to the embeddedness of all human action within a wider range of social processes as the "stratified nature of social reality. Even the most mundane actions make sense only because they contain in-built assumptions about a wider set of social rules and institutions" (Pawson & Tilley, 1997a, p. 406). Theoretical and experimental work seek to establish the existence and properties of these structures and construct confirmable explanatory theories about these structures and their properties. Different disciplines and different investigators may organize their apprehension of phenomena differently; however, the perspectives that guide any scientific study must be made explicit.

Rather than concentrate on events and the linking of variables at the surface (for example, the mere establishment of cause-and-effect relationships between the intervention and its effects), scientific realism addresses the questions of why a program works, for whom, and in what circumstances. The perspective is holistic. With such a perspective a social work researcher may be more aware of the limitations of the research attempted, of its exact contribution to the whole, and of what needs to be addressed in the future. Like pragmatism, scientific realism is wholeheartedly methodological-pluralist; unlike pragmatism, however, the evaluator not only responds to the needs of practice in order to judge it but also retains a holistic approach to reality in order to improve practice.

As a perspective of research into practice, scientific realism can address four key concerns for practitioners:

1. How to select a model of intervention
2. How to use effectiveness research in the selection process
3. How to target the intervention in pre-existing contexts
4. How to improve the intervention models based on evaluation research.

Scientific realism is based on a scientific approach to the construction of models of intervention. Unlike empirical practice, which has no account of the content of theories to be tested, the realist scientific schema has a rational process for the invention of theories:

> there are ideal forms of reasoning at work in that area of human thinking too. They have to do with the canons of constructing and imagining models, and thus depend upon principles governing the rational way to make comparisons, to judge likenesses against unlikenesses. They lead to areas of structure more complex than the deductive relationships that are to be found at work in the organized parts of mathematics. (Harre, 1984, pp. 57–58)

Scientific researchers build models in an attempt to apprehend the realities, then—on the basis of comparisons as approximations of reality—improve the models. A dialectic relationship exists between the construction of the model and its analogous comparisons with reality.

In social work, practitioners construct models in their practices that include the practitioners' theoretical orientations, practice wisdom, accepted knowledge among peers, tacit knowledge, and previous experiences of what works, for whom, and in what contexts. Starting with the existing model (Figure 3.2), the practitioner makes an assessment (in partnership with the client) that leads to hypotheses about what might work, for whom, and in what contexts. Then, through observation and other multiple-method data gathering of information about the pre-existing mechanisms, contexts, and outcomes, the practitioner is able to make the intervention program more specific and to aim it in a way that harnesses enabling mechanisms and avoids disabling mechanisms.

At this stage, the multiple-method data gathering addresses the questions of what actually works, for whom, and in what contexts. In a realist effectiveness cycle, all the data feed back into the theory that we started from. In this way, evaluation research is about improving the construction of models, and therefore about improving the content of the practice itself. Evidence is used to focus program content so that it can stimulate the desired changes in pre-existing mechanisms and contexts. As a byproduct, the evidence can be used to prove the program's effectiveness and to make judgments about its effectiveness; however, the main purpose of evidence-gathering is to improve the model. Objectivity lies not just in the use of measures, but in the extent to which the model is analogous to reality. At each cycle, a better approximation of reality is obtained. In this way,

Figure 3.2.

Realist Effectiveness Cycle. Adapted from Pawson & Tilley, 1997.

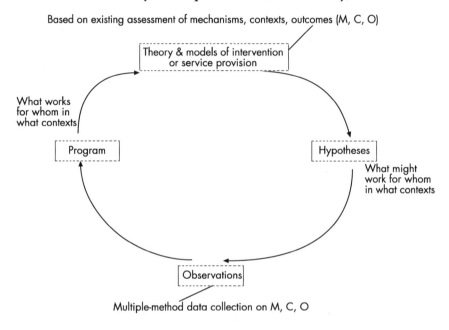

scientific realism addresses all the dimensions and questions of practice effectiveness that other schema cannot—including content, outcomes, the perceptions of all the people involved, ethics, values, and contexts.

The rules of scientific realism include addressing the following elements:

- how and why a program has the potential to cause change
- how it informs and alters choices that people make
- how causal mechanisms for problems are countered by the program's alternative causal mechanisms
- how problem mechanisms are activated in contexts
- how a generative mechanism (the program of intervention) can be started successfully
- what the outcomes are and how they are produced.

Realism addresses the real structures or context-mechanism-outcome configurations, and the questions of what works, for whom, and in what circumstances, to improve future practice or the construction of future models of good practice.

CONTRIBUTION OF SCIENTIFIC REALISM

The other main paradigms in contemporary British social work practice research—empirical practice, pragmatism, and critical theory—offer their own contributions to the theory and practice of effectiveness research. As a worldview there are limitations in each of these approaches, and they tend to emphasize one or the other parts of the real entities in which social work operates. Therefore, they fail to address the complexities of social work in a holistic way, and their main purpose tends to be making judgments of past practice with the hope of influencing future practice. The scientific realist approach, on the other hand, encourages the researcher to seek a wider view of effectiveness in an attempt to apprehend the complex reality of social work practice as it is. Based on the construction and testing of models of practice, this approach not only enables judgments to be made about past practice, but also is inextricably linked to improving future practice.

The social worker constructs a model that attempts to explain reality, and based on this explanation, aims to change reality. Depending on the ethics and values underpinning practice, this model may be constructed in partnership with the service user, in keeping with the enabling role of the social worker. Other influences on the construction of the model include tacit knowledge and practice wisdom; previous experience of the effectiveness of other models, in a variety of contexts; and agency policies, political pressures, perspectives of other professionals, and perspectives of relevant others. The model includes assessments of personal, social, and environmental difficulties; a program of intervention designed to help through supportive, rehabilitative, protective, or corrective action; and expectations of changes.

In other words, realist effectiveness research must take into account the social worker's model as a whole—its study of the interacting mechanisms and the contexts that have given rise to the client's difficulties, the potential enabling and disabling mechanisms, and the accuracy in the starting of the generative mechanism (or the content and the targeting of the intervention). Furthermore, the model cannot be seen as a static entity that is tested over a period of time and then subsequently judged on its success. If it is going to be effective in a generative sense, the model must change in accordance with changes in the complex weave of mechanisms and contexts. The theory, the assessment, the intervention, and the outcomes all change in the fluid contexts of reality. Therefore, effectiveness is not about past performance.

Collected evidence may provide information about the model's effectiveness—its accuracy, effect on other mechanisms, or effect on contexts—but, as we stated before, this is a by-product. The central purposes of the evidence are to improve the program's content and targeting, to improve the theory, to improve the assessment, and thereby to improve the mix of data gathering techniques in a continuous cycle of improvement.

An important contribution of scientific realism is that it is inclusive of all the other perspectives considered in this chapter (with the exception of postmodernist relativism). A new perspective in social work practice research, the scientific realist perspective is now being applied and tested. As yet, no published examples exist, and therefore as far as its limitations are concerned, the jury is still out. Now that the stall of fallibilistic realism has been set out, those who follow this paradigm should clearly state their position, and demonstrate the products of effectiveness research for the scrutiny of others. At the same time, researchers who are at the boundaries should clarify their ontological and epistemological positions, to enable such scrutiny to take place in further critical analyses of this and other contemporary paradigmatic influences in British social work.

Conclusion

This chapter has presented the main perspectives in contemporary social work practice research in England, including an analysis of their contributions and limitations. Each of the perspectives included here—empirical practice, pragmatism, critical theory and scientific realism—has an important role to play in addressing the complexities of practice, and each sets out to achieve this goal in its own way. Adapting Michael Scriven's terminology of black, gray, and white box evaluations (Scriven, 1994), black box evaluation is where the researcher concentrates on evaluating a program's effects without addressing the components that make up the program. Such research is crucially important, and stands in its own right—this is the role of much empirical practice research. In a gray box evaluation the components of a program are discerned, but their inner workings or principles of operation are not fully revealed—this is the contribution of much pragmatic and critical theorist research.

In the last year, a new perspective—scientific realism—has entered social work. This perspective, which brings together almost all of the other main perspectives, attempts a white box evaluation of practice, addressing the effects, the inner workings and operations of the components of the program, and how they are connected. It attempts to reveal not only what works in social work practice, but also what works for whom, and in what contexts. Scientific realism is nirvana for evidence-based practice. To reach this bliss, we at the Centre for Evaluation Studies at the University of Huddersfield now are conducting several research projects with social workers who are rising to the challenge.

References

Anastas, J. W., & MacDonald, M. L. (1994). *Research design for social work and the human services.* New York: Lexington Books.

Bhaskar, R. (1978). *A realist theory of science* (2nd ed.). Brighton, England: Harvester.

Bryman, A. (1988). *Quantity and quality in social research.* London: Unwin Hyman.

Central Council for Education and Training in Social Work (CCETSW). (1989). *Requirements and regulations for the Diploma in Social Work.* Paper no. 30. London: Author.

Cheetham, J. (1998). The evaluation of social work: Priorities, problems and possibilities. In J. Cheetham & M. A. F. Kazi (Eds.), *The working of social work.* London: Jessica Kingsley.

Cheetham, J., Fuller, R., McIvor, G., & Petch, A. (1992). *Evaluating social work effectiveness.* Buckingham, England: Open University Press.

Everitt, A., & Hardiker, P. (1996). *Evaluating for good practice.* Basingstoke, England: Macmillan.

Fischer, J., & Corcoran, K. (1994). *Measures for clinical practice: A source book* (Vols. 1 & 2). New York: Free Press.

Fraser, M., Taylor, M. J., Jackson, R., & O'Jack, J. (1991). Social work and science: Many ways of knowing? *Social Work Research & Abstracts, 27,* 5–15.

Fuller, R. (1996). Evaluating social work effectiveness: A pragmatic approach. In P. Alderson, S. Brill, I. Chalmers, R. Fuller, P. Hinkley-Smith, G. Macdonald, T. Newman, A. Oakley, H. Roberts, & H. Ward (Eds.), *What works? Effective social interventions in child welfare* (pp. 55–67). Ilford, England: Barnardo's.

Fuller, R., & Petch, A. (1995). *Practitioner research: The reflexive social worker.* Buckingham, England: Open University Press.

Guba, E. G. (1990). The alternative paradigm dialog. In E. G. Guba (Ed.), *The paradigm dialog* (pp. 17–27). Thousand Oaks, CA: Sage.

Harre, R. (1984). *The philosophies of science: An introductory survey* (2nd ed.). Oxford: Oxford University Press.

Jordan, B. (1978). A comment on "theory and practice in social work." *British Journal of Social Work, 8,* 23–25.

Kazi, M.A.F. (1998). *Single-case evaluation for social workers.* Aldershot, England: Averbury.

Kazi, M.A.F. (1998). Putting single-case evaluation into practice. In J. Cheetham & M. A. F. Kazi (Eds.), *The working of social work* (pp. 187–199). London: Jessica Kingsley.

Kazi, M.A.F. (1997). Single-case evaluation in British social services. In E. Chelimsky & W. R. Shadish (Eds.), *Evaluation for the 21st Century: A resource book* (pp. 419–442). Thousand Oaks, CA: Sage.

Kazi, M.A.F. (1997, March). *Toward a pragmatic approach to the proper method mix.* Paper presented at the 1997 European Evaluation Society Conference "Evaluation: What Works and for Whom?", Stockholm.

Kazi, M.A.F. (1996). The Centre for Evaluation Studies at the University of Huddersfield: A profile. *Research on Social Work Practice, 6,* 104–116.

Kazi, M.A.F., Mantysaari, M., & Rostila, I. (1997). Promoting the use of single-case designs: Social work experiences from England and Finland. *Research on Social Work Practice, 7,* 311–328.

Layder, D. (1993). *New strategies in social research.* Cambridge: Polity Press.

Macdonald, G. (1996). Ice therapy: Why we need randomised controlled trials. In P. Alderson, S. Brill, I. Chalmers, R. Fuller, P. Hinkley-Smith, G. Macdonald, T. Newman, A. Oakley, H. Roberts, & H. Ward (Eds.), *What works? Effective social interventions in child welfare* (pp. 16–32). Ilford, England: Barnardo's.

Manicas, P. T. (1987). *A history and philosophy of the social sciences.* Oxford: Basil Blackwell.

Manicas, P. T., & Secord, P. F. (1983). Implications for psychology of the new philosophy of science. *American Psychologist, 38,* 399–413.

Martin, L. L., & Kettner, P. M. (1996). *Measuring the performance of human service programs.* Thousand Oaks, CA: Sage.

Medawar, P. (1982). *Pluto's Republic.* Oxford: Oxford University Press.

Myers, L. L., & Thyer, B. A. (1997). Should social work clients have the right to effective treatment? *Social Work, 42,* 288–298.

Oakley, A. (1996). Who's afraid of the randomised controlled trial? The challenge of evaluating the potential of social interventions. In P. Alderson, S. Brill, I. Chalmers, R. Fuller, P. Hinkley-Smith, G. Macdonald, T. Newman, A. Oakley, H. Roberts, & H. Ward (Eds.), *What works? Effective social interventions in child welfare* (pp. 33–47). Ilford, England: Barnardo's.

Outhwaite, W. (1987). *New philosophies of social science: Realism, hermeneutics and critical theory.* London: Macmillan.

Parton, N. (1994). "Problematics of government": (post) modernity and social work. *British Journal of Social Work, 24,* 9–32.

Pawson, R., & Tilley, N. (1997a). An introduction to scientific realist evaluation. In E. Chelimsky & W. R. Shadish (Eds.), *Evaluation for the 21st Century: A resource book* (pp. 405–418). Thousand Oaks, CA: Sage.

Pawson, R., & Tilley, N. (1997b). *Realistic evaluation.* Thousand Oaks, CA: Sage.

Petch, A. (1992). *At home in the community.* Aldershot: Averbury.

Phillips, D. C. (1990). Postpositivistic science: Myths and realities. In E. G. Guba (Ed.), *The paradigm dialog* (pp. 31–45). Thousand Oaks, CA: Sage.

Popkewitz, T. S. (1990). Whose future? Whose past? Notes on critical theory and methodology. In E. G. Guba (Ed.), *The paradigm dialog* (pp. 46–66). Thousand Oaks, CA: Sage.

Scriven, M. (1994). The fine line between evaluation and explanation. *Evaluation Practice, 15,* 75–77.

Shaw, I. (1996). *Evaluating in practice.* Aldershot, England: Arena.

Shaw, I. (1998). Practising evaluation. In J. Cheetham & M. A. F. Kazi (Eds.), *The working of social work* (pp. 201–223). London: Jessica Kingsley.

Sheldon, B. (1978). Theory and practice in social work: A re-examination of a tenuous relationship. *British Journal of Social Work, 8,* 1–22.

Thyer, B. A. (1993). Social work theory and practice research: The approach of logical positivism. *Social Work & Social Sciences Review, 4,* 5–26.

Trinder, L. (1996). Social work research: The state of the art (or science). *Child & Family Social Work, 1,* 233–242.

Tyson, K. B. (1992). A new approach to relevant scientific research for practitioners: The heuristic paradigm. *Social Work, 37,* 541–556.

CHAPTER 4

Practitioner Research: Toward Reflexive Practice?

Roger Fuller

At first sight the notion of practitioner research in social work does not seem altogether promising. Social workers themselves are often portrayed as hostile to research, their own experiences of it leading them to see it as "sociological sadism" (Shaw, 1996) and something imposed on them from outside. The imposition may come literally from outside the institution (for example, researchers descending on a social work department from the university, often at the behest of a remote senior management or an even more remote government department); or from conceptually outside (researchers seen as operating from a value base alien to that of a profession that places a high estimation on its own values). A number of stereotypes may be invoked: researchers as careerists making their academic reputations out of the human miseries that pervade daily life in a social work setting; researchers as remorseless quantifiers of the infinite diversity of individual distress, or as hatchet-men and hatchet-women for cost-conscious policymakers. Such caricatures are not confined to one side. Social workers are, it is often said, innumerate, careless of empirical evidence about the effectiveness of their efforts, resistant to evaluation, and prone to persisting with personal preference at the expense of "evidence-based practice." The profession has been assailed for these tendencies, even by voices friendly to social work (Macdonald, 1995; Macdonald & Sheldon, 1992).

And yet in the eleven years I have spent at the Social Work Research Centre (SWRC) in Scotland, in an academically based unit devoted to studying social work policy and practice, I have not found this picture to be true—or at least not uniformly or universally so. This period has seen the development of a wide range of pressures on social work to be more generally accountable. It has also seen the publication of a number of texts featuring the concept of "practitioner research," including our own (for example, Broad & Fletcher, 1993; Edwards & Talbot, 1994; Fuller & Petch, 1995; Whittaker & Archer, 1989). This chapter describes the attempt we have made at Stirling to foster the development of research-minded practice, in the shape of what we have called the Practitioner Research Programme. However, I will first look briefly at the dimensions, in part paradoxical, of research's uneasy relationship to social work practice.

Research and Practice

Neither social work nor research is monolithic. The following attempt to sum up general trends is therefore hazardous. In recent years social work services in the United Kingdom have changed significantly in terms of their organization and structure. When I first began researching social care some 25 years ago, social work took place in generic area teams or residential settings. Beyond these settings the practice of social work was relatively undifferentiated: people "did" social work. Along with parallel developments in other social work areas, the community care legislation of 1991 confirmed a longstanding trend toward specialization, and both formalized and pushed further a considerable disaggregation of social work activities. Since then social work in the UK has tended to be organized broadly into adult services, child care and protection, and (in Scotland) criminal justice. The traditional roles of social work have been further broken down into, for example, the assessment and care management tasks of screening, care planning, monitoring, and review. Some researchers and practitioners have wondered whether the term *social worker* is itself at risk and likely to give way to labels like *care manager* or *child protection officer*. At the same time managerial influences and concepts have grown, as seen in a proliferation of the language of objectives, targeting, standards, performance review, quality assurance, best value, and the like. Politically encouraged diversification of service provision, with more use of the voluntary and private sectors (the mixed economy), has given rise to a contract culture with the development of purchaser-provider splits and service commissioning. All of these trends have been accompanied by consumerist approaches and a statutory obligation to obtain consumer views in the planning and delivery of services. A research—or at least measurement—flavor permeates many of these activities. Even more pronounced is the accompanying stress on service evaluation, most obviously seen in the United Kingdom in what has become known as the "what works?" movement in offender services and services to children, and in the advocacy of evidence-based practice.

Bruised and battered as they perennially are by ill-informed public criticism, social workers may see many of these trends as threatening to the values they have traditionally placed on respect for individuals. And some of these trends no doubt constitute such a threat. At the same time, and in interaction with changes in the character and politics of social work, developments have occurred in the kinds of issues addressed by social work research. In my professional lifetime broad emphases in social work–related research have moved first from studies of client need and of social work organization to evaluative work. More recently, in a period when social workers are as likely to be blamed for social problems as to be seen as the means of solving them, increasing emphasis has been placed on critically inspired studies. British and European academic and political circles have paid particular attention recently to the concept of social exclusion (see, for example, the chapters in Barry & Hallett, forthcoming). Such studies bring to the foreground the perspectives of excluded or marginalized groups, may seek to involve them in agenda-setting and the research process, and may seek to champion their rights to empowering processes of service delivery, leading to their social inclusion and treatment as full citizens. This has happened most clearly in the case of people with physical disabilities, survivors of psychiatric illnesses, and people with learning disabilities, and it is beginning to happen with older people and children. It is hard to quarrel with such a trend, but a personal view of these developments would be that there may be some danger that social workers and their concerns— so often the "middle people"—might be squeezed out between a top-down managerial research agenda and a bottom-up user-centered critique.

SWRC has been influenced by these movements. It was initially established with an evaluative mission. Within social work evaluation in the United Kingdom, some researchers have espoused the randomized controlled trial (RCT) as the gold standard (Macdonald & Sheldon, 1992), while others have opted for the disciplined pragmatism of method associated with SWRC (Cheetham et al., 1992).

In adopting a pragmatic and eclectic approach to evaluation, without being blind to its inadequacies, we were influenced by our early experience in constructing viable research designs appropriate for addressing specific issues. Academic debates about epistemology or methodology have not been particularly well developed in the United Kingdom in our field, beyond some rather empty arguments for and against positivism. Broadly speaking, SWRC in its evaluative phase pursued no single method while developing programs of research in community care, social work and criminal justice, and children's and youths' issues. As one of the few academic research units in the United Kingdom dedicated exclusively to *social work* (which we have always defined broadly), SWRC has had a certain influence, particularly in Scotland. We also have occupied a rather exposed position, and have been criticized (Trinder, 1996) both for being too positivist and—though not by many—for not being positivist enough. More recent development at SWRC has mirrored that elsewhere in the United Kingdom, with movement away from straight evaluation and a direct focus on social work toward a more critical stance, a focus on service users, and an interest in the broader welfare context of social work services.

Amid these shifting patterns research has loomed larger in UK social work during the last decade. Its impact has been felt in a variety of ways. Successive legislation has been significantly influenced by research findings (the Children Act of 1989, the introduction of community care, the Children [Scotland] Act of 1995). The proliferation of research-related concepts like performance indicators has been noted above. Justified demands for professional accountability have been prompted by both external criticisms and a growing realization that research has produced positive findings for social work effectiveness (Macdonald & Sheldon, 1992). And both the British Association of Social Workers (BASW) and the Central Council for the Education and Training of Social Workers (CCETSW, 1989 and its successors) have endorsed research and evaluation as important elements in the professional repertoire of social workers.

At the very least, and perhaps in a somewhat defensive spirit, there is a case for social workers to develop a degree of research mindedness as a way to understand some of the pressures brought to bear on social work. This perspective may provide social workers a means of critically responding to the demands made on them by legislation and by the general movement toward greater accountability to communities and users. "Research mindedness" has a number of components, including the following:

· an awareness of the scope and limitations of research
· an ability to read critically the claims that emerge from research studies
· an ability to read critically the policy changes that purport to be based on research studies
· a sympathetic attitude toward research that may be conducted in a practitioner's own work setting.

More positively, Everitt et al. (1992) see the development of research awareness among practitioners as a means of reclaiming professionalism, of asserting the value, and values, of the professional discipline of social work over and against the limiting features of its bureaucratic and ideological setting. From this perspective, the research-minded practitioner is seen as a more complete professional, better able to challenge organizational or political constraints, more aware of the social structures that underlie the kinds of difficulties experienced by clients, and more skeptical of taken-for-granted features of the world of social work. Practitioners also will develop a research appreciation capacity, enabling them to read research both more receptively and more critically, and to make use of it in thinking about implications for their own practice or about agency policies (Black, 1993). If practitioners are to be encouraged to take research into account in pondering issues of practice or management, they must be able to distinguish the rigorous from the weak and the relevant from the irrelevant in research reports.

There is, finally, the pragmatic consideration that social workers now find themselves under considerable pressure to demonstrate their effectiveness at the tasks allotted to them by a sometimes dubious political process. Therefore, if social workers fail to involve themselves in carrying out the required research, it will be done by others who may be less sympathetic to the nature of those tasks. There are questions here of the social status of the social work profession, whose relatively low standing in the eyes of key constituencies (as compared, say, with the medical professions) probably stems at least in part from its failure thus far to develop a social work equivalent to the tradition of clinical research.

Developing Research-Minded Practice

Having identified making practice more research-minded as a legitimate aim, we might have pursued that aim in a number of ways. Options included the following actions:

- contributing actively to teaching research components in initial qualifying programs
- organizing seminars and conferences for practitioners on research skills
- creating fora whereby research agendas could be influenced by practitioners and managers
- organizing research studies (where practicable) in ways that permitted early feedback of results
- focusing dissemination efforts on practice audiences.

We explored all of these approaches with varying amounts of energy and discovered that all have their pros and cons. At the same time we often received requests for help or advice, usually on short notice, and especially in situations where a project's funding depended on its being at least seen to incorporate evaluation. These numerous requests from the field for short-term evaluations often were difficult to respond to in a helpful way. At some point the thought occurred—why not teach them to do it themselves? In particular, why not devise a program that would see people through the processes of carrying out a study from start to finish?

Initially filled with trepidation, we were genuinely uncertain whether such a program would work. Given that any program we could mount could make only limited demands of agencies' time-pressed staff, would participants be able to achieve anything worthy of the name "research"? Would anyone want to do it? If they did, would they stay the course, or would disillusion and attrition be common? Could we achieve sufficient knowledge transfer to seriously affect people's thinking and their subsequent practice?

Figure 4.1.

Practitioner Research Programme

September   Residential course   Introduction to research concepts
                 (3 days)   Methodological repertoire
                                          Research plan

                                          Finalize plan
                                          Piloting
                                          Identify sample

February   Recall day   Data analysis
                                          Problem solving

                                          Data collection
                                          Analysis
                                          Preliminary report

June   Residential course   Problem solving
                 (2 days)   Writing
                                          Dissemination plan
                                          Review

STIRLING'S PRACTITIONER RESEARCH PROGRAMME

Initial funding was obtained from the Joseph Rowntree Foundation, and we obtained support in principle from The Scottish Office, the Association of Directors of Social Work, and from the British Association of Social Workers. A program was advertised. Applicants had to convince us that they had a viable idea for a study based in their own agency, and that they had management approval for the time they would need to devote to it. We selected 20 participants. Figure 4.1 outlines the program structure, which was developed initially by Alison Petch and myself, and which has remained in much the same form.

In the first three-day course, teaching took place in plenary, small-group, and individual sessions. Each participant was allocated an individual advisor. Our objectives were to demystify some key research concepts, display examples of different research designs and methods, and (most importantly) develop for each participant a detailed research plan. The research plan was to incorporate researchable questions, specification of the sample, methods, and an accompanying timetable. Produced in poster form for the group to share, the plan was to be revised after discussion and agreed on with advisors in the fortnight following the residential course.

During the next nine months, participants' studies progressed through their successive stages, with regular telephone consultations with advisors. We soon learned to give clear direction, usually in the form of setting staging posts for the development of instruments; piloting, identification and recruitment of samples; data collection; and analysis. Halfway through this period, the group reconvened for a day to share and solve problems, receive further input on analysis, and (we found) recharge any fading motivation or resolve.

Participants were asked to submit a short preliminary report before the final two-day session. Each participant made a 15-minute presentation to the group, the importance of dissemination was stressed, and advice was given on targeting dissemination efforts and forming a dissemination plan. Deadlines were set for the completion of a final summary report to be submitted following a prescribed format and a full report to be submitted in a format determined by the individual on the basis of the particular dissemination purposes. We have published collections of the summary reports (for example, SWRC, 1993) and disseminated them widely.

A controversial feature of the program was that the final product was not formally assessed. This considered (but finely balanced) decision meant that the participants were entirely self-motivated, and that they did not have to meet any bureaucratic requirements extrinsic to the purposes of their particular studies—or to the uses they might wish to make of them. It also meant, however, that standards were uncertain and that some participants could feel a little cheated at the end, with nothing tangible to show.

The Participants and Their Topics

We have found that the ideal number of participants for each cohort is about 20, which provides scope for small groups of people with similar areas of interest to benefit from each others' experiences. Since the program started in 1991, some 80 to 100 practitioners have taken part in successive programs. Most participants have come from local authority social work departments, with a significant minority from the voluntary sector. Program participants have studied a wide range of topics across the spectrum of the main social work services. Typical titles studied include

- An Evaluation of Community Service Orders from the User's Perspective
- Needs of Hearing Impaired People in Residential Homes for Older People
- Care Giver Support Groups: A Comparative Study
- Relative Stress in Different Social Work Settings
- The Relationship between Care Giver and Parent in Day Care for Young Children.

Some division has occurred between those who have addressed mainstream research questions, those concerned with evaluating projects in their own local communities, and those whose studies stemmed from quite personal and particular interests. Mainstream studies have sometimes echoed those in SWRC's own research program (for example, fostering breakdown rates, or factors associated with the successful completion of community service orders). Studies with a local focus often have applied case-study style methods that have been used elsewhere on a larger canvas. And the third group addressed topics that do not always get on to academic research agendas (for example, the role of social work with personality-disordered clients, or with clients with eating disorders). A general impression has been that the more interesting work is offered by the latter two groups, who bring their own local activities and personal enthusiasms into focus rather than try to ape larger and better-resourced studies.

Relationship to Agency Research Agendas

We hoped that agencies would take note of the research interest of their employees and consciously use it in their own plans for developing their research base. Perhaps predictably, this was the exception rather than the rule; however, it did occur in the larger agencies with well-established in-house research units. In this sense, the effect of the program has been uncertain. When the initial funding expired and agencies began to pay fees for the employees to participate, we wondered whether participants would be placed under more pressure to investigate topics suited to agency agendas, or even to manipulate their findings in the interests of departmental image. We have found no evidence that this happened. Any tension between the interests of the individual research-minded professional and the agenda of the employing agency has been latent rather than manifest. While this lack of imposition has been encouraging, it could also be taken as a dispiriting illustration of the low esteem in which research is held in social work practice agencies.

Participants' Support Needs

We had expected that our main difficulties would lie in the feasibility of transferring sufficient conceptual understanding and technical knowledge, by a short course and through advisors, to make for a viable product. This was indeed an issue. The priorities of the program have been:

- the formulation of specific researchable questions
- the appropriateness for different tasks, and the logistics and time implications, of different kinds of data and ways of collecting them
- the techniques, logistics and time implications of different approaches to analysis
- the importance and range of methods of disseminating findings.

The importance of each item was self-evident, especially the first: Starting with inappropriately formulated research questions swiftly leads to failure and disillusion. Most of the feedback we received from participants, however, suggested that the main problem they encountered was more mundane: that of finding adequate time. Although the conditions of participation had specified that some amount of protected time in the practitioner's workplace should be agreed on with managers, it became evident that not all such agreements were adhered to. This problem was one of the main causes of failure to complete the program (although the rate of such failure remained at an acceptably low level). It is difficult to convey adequately in advance the fact that much of the necessary time has to be quality time, without distraction.

Participants also testified to the importance of moral as well as technical support. Research can be a lonely undertaking, and studies frequently do not proceed according to plan. Study advisors must steer an important but delicate course between prescription as to deadlines and encouragement. Participants also gained vital moral support from a group of peers experiencing similar problems. We encouraged participants to develop partnerships or "pairs" with another group member, that might potentially extend to the mutual exchange of research assistance; and although such arrangements were uncommon, they were beneficial when they worked, and social contacts often survived the program.

Methods

Clearly a program like this has insufficient teaching time to do justice to the full range of methods, and insufficient research time for ambitious data collection strategies. We had to challenge a number of myths believed in by participants who had no research experience—for example, that research needs large samples and statistical expertise, that it is invariably necessary to have a control group, and that samples must always be representative. Our general approach was to recommend simple, tried-and-tested methods and to counsel wariness about inventing new methods or instruments. We stressed the importance of building into research designs a comparative dimension, and pointed out the scope and limits to what can be said on the basis of the main social science data collection methods (questionnaires, interviews, scales, secondary data, diaries, observation, and so on). We also found it was important to spell out the logistical implications—the nuts and bolts—of opting for particular methods.

Despite our mild discouragement of innovative methods (in the interests of getting the job successfully completed on time), some participants have demonstrated methodological imagination in (for example) the use of videos and in enterprising combinations of different methods. Our expectation was that practitioners, likely confident in the basic toolkit of social work practice, would most often choose to carry out interview-based studies. This expectation was only partially borne out, as several have drawn on departmental records or used secondary analysis of data from existing surveys to construct quite large samples. The characteristic study, however, has been the small interviewing exercise involving users, carers, or fellow professionals, with small sample sizes. It has therefore been particularly important to establish with participants (not always with complete success) the difference between a research study and a series of cozy chats! The vulnerabilities of this approach lead to a challenging question, which admirers of the program have been (to our surprise) somewhat slow to raise: Is this really research?

Is This Really Research?

This question is complicated by the lack of formal assessment. Any answer clearly turns on what the questioner might understand by the term research, or on how much one thinks that it matters. I take a fairly relaxed view of this, although some social work professionals may consider this heretical. Beyond a core process of systematic inquiry into clearly defined questions, gathering material that will throw some light on those questions, and reporting on it, there are many views of the defining characteristics of research. I have no intention here of attempting to settle age-old disputes. The cause of research-minded practice would be ill served if participants came away with the notions that theory is of no account, that the validity of statements is unaffected by method, sample size, or sample composition, or that the shortcuts taken (given the program's constraints of time and resources) are free of intellectual cost. It is, however, perfectly normal practice in research to accept trade-offs between the demands of theoretical and methodological purism and what is feasible. Given the circumstances of practitioner research, the research advisor's role in safeguarding the integrity of the participants' efforts is a skilled and intellectually responsible one.

Whatever their status as research, practitioner studies are necessarily small-scale and local. Some years ago, we (Cheetham et al., 1992) wrote of the value of modest studies:

> Small studies may . . . be either particularly appropriate or, indeed the only sensible option in certain situations. These include agencies' need to gain some swift, albeit impressionistic, understanding of the immediate impact of new legislation on certain user groups or on the operation of services. Innovative projects, or those using very unusual forms of intervention, may also best be examined by small studies, perhaps to test the feasibility of longer comparative research. . . . Small studies of individual or team practice can encourage the critical evaluation of services, particularly when they become a regular feature of agencies' approach to their work. (pp. 143–144)

It must be said that the program has, inevitably, produced research of variable quality. Judged by the standards with which academics are familiar, the best studies have been of something approaching master's degree standard, albeit shorn of the literature review and epistemological argumentation that sometimes disfigures dissertations. Other studies have been more ephemeral. Many participants have assured us that, for them, the process has been as important as the product. Participants have given us examples of the ways their experience of practitioner research has affected their approach to practice:

- [It] has helped maintain my interest in my practice and continue questioning and developing how we work.
- I particularly enjoyed the direct link between real practice development and research. . . . I find it easier to think in evaluative terms, or to prompt questions that may lead to a research proposal.
- [The] PRP gave me confidence—research was possible for ordinary practitioners and not something "out there" for people in ivory towers.
- The PRP gives status to practitioners by recognizing the importance of the issues they face.
- We approach (the research section) for advice whereas before we may have seen them as rather elite or our own questions as rather trivial.
- Research is addictive. . . .

Some participants have published their work in journals or spoken at conferences. A few have even deserted practice for full-time research—which is one kind of tribute to the program, but rather subverts its objectives!

Toward Reflexive Practice

We have found that practitioners bring certain advantages to the research task. They also need to overcome certain pitfalls. Advantages include an overlap in professional skills. Research-minded practitioners are well placed to inform research agendas, as they know better than most what questions could be addressed to increase understanding of the circumstances and problems of communities and service users, and to improve service effectiveness. They have well-developed skills of problem analysis, interviewing, recording, and filtering out the irrelevant. They often have better access to data than the external researcher. They need to distance themselves from many of their day-to-day assumptions, however, to seek help in the formulation of questions, to realize that the researcher's relationship with a client has a different focus than that of the social worker. Practitioners must also be prepared for the conflicts of allegiance and responsibility to colleagues and the agency that can come from switching between the roles of researcher and practitioner. If the advantages can be capitalized on and the traps avoided, research skills can make more systematic and informed such basic social work tasks as gathering and collating information about individual clients, assessing resources and their likely efficacy, monitoring progress and evaluating effectiveness, and feeding information to service planners and policymakers.

"Reflexive practice" (after Schön, 1983, slightly but significantly amended; Fuller & Petch, 1995)—a practice that is capable of learning from experience and adapting itself to the lessons learned—is a seductive concept, easier to proclaim than to substantiate. It is best described by anecdote. Consider, for example, a practitioner who notices apparent changes over time in the character of referrals; who explores whether the changes are real; who consults with colleagues and compares notes; who checks out available sources of information (whether locally or by going further afield for enlightenment as to possible reasons); who can evaluate whether researchable issues have been unearthed by these inquiries; and who then can make suggestions in appropriate quarters or even carry out a piece of research—this practitioner displays research-minded reflexivity.

I do not wish to make large claims for the venture described here. Our program can affect only a small minority of the workforce; and to have more than a minor effect on the manifold forces guiding the development of social work in Scotland is beyond its scope. Currently the program is in abeyance pending consideration of ways of strengthening its base and increasing its effect in the field. A priority is the need to persuade agencies to give more than lip service to the desirability and potential usefulness of research-minded practice. This is a struggle to be waged on several fronts, including

· the strengthening and appropriate uses of in-house research capacities
· the fostering of a range of modes of partnership between academic and practice institutions
· the developing of a research-literate senior management in productive dialogue with those who set research agendas.

There is more than one way of interesting practitioners in research and more than one way of "keeping social work honest" (Shaw & Shaw, 1998).

The circumstances in which we were able to develop this program—a core-funded research unit prepared to devote time to an activity that carries few academic kudos—are likely to be unusual.

These caveats having been made, practitioner research of the kind described here can play a significant role in the future of social work. This chapter has broadly argued that practitioners should and can be involved in research; that such involvement makes a modest contribution toward overcoming the damaging mutual mistrust that can exist between the worlds of research and of social work practice; and that practitioner research is an important means of promoting research awareness among practitioners and a more informed practice discourse in agencies. The Scottish experience shows that it can be done.

References

Barry, M., & Hallett, C. (Eds.) (1998). *Social exclusion and social work: Issues of theory, policy, and practice.* Lyme Regis, England: Russell House Publishing.

Black, T. R. (1993). *Evaluating social science research.* London: Sage.

Broad, B., & Fletcher, C. (Eds.) (1993). *Practitioner social work research in action.* London: Whiting & Birch.

Central Council for Education and Training of Social Workers (1989). *Requirements and regulations for the Diploma in Social Work.* Paper No. 30. London: Author.

Cheetham, J., Fuller, R., McIvor, G., & Petch, A. (1993). *Evaluating social work effectiveness.* Buckingham, England: Open University Press.

Connor, A. (1993). *Monitoring and evaluation made easy: A handbook for voluntary organisations.* Edinburgh: HMSO.

Edwards, A., & Talbot, R. (1994) *The hard-pressed researcher.* London: Longman.

Everitt, A., Hardiker, P., Littlewood, J., & Mullender, A. (1992). *Applied research for better practice.* London: Macmillan.

Fuller, R., & Petch, A. (1995). *Practitioner research: The reflexive social worker.* Buckingham, England: Open University Press.

Macdonald, G. (1996). Ice therapy: Why we need randomised controlled trials. In T. Newman & H. Roberts (Eds.), *What works? Effective social interventions in child welfare* (pp. 16–32). Ilford, England: Barnardo's.

Macdonald, G., & Sheldon, B. (1992). Contemporary studies of the effectiveness of social work. *British Journal of Social Work, 22,* 615–644.

Robson, C. (1993). *Real world research.* Oxford: Blackwell.

Schön, D. (1983). *The reflective practitioner: How professionals think in action.* London: Temple Smith.

Shaw, I. (1996). *Evaluating in practice.* Aldershot, England: Arena.

Shaw, I., & Shaw, A. (1998). Keeping social work honest: Evaluating as profession and practice. *British Journal of Social Work, 27,* 847–869.

Social Work Research Centre (1993). *Practitioner Research Programme 1993–1994: Summary Reports.* Stirling, Scotland: University of Stirling.

Trinder, L. (1996). Social work research: The state of the art (or science). *Child and Family Social Work, 1,* 233–242.

Whitaker, D. S., & Archer, J. L. (1989). *Research by social workers: Capitalizing on experience.* London: Central Council for Education and Training of Social Workers.

CHAPTER 5

Progress in the Development of Research Resources in Social Work

David M. Austin

T he Task Force on Social Work Research, appointed in 1988 by Lewis Judd, MD, Director of the National Institute of Mental Health (NIMH), presented a report to the National Advisory Mental Health Council of NIMH in December of 1991. That report, *Building Social Work Knowledge for Effective Services and Policies—A Plan for Research Development,* was based on an extensive assessment of the research resources in the field of social work and the requirements for strengthening those resources to contribute to the social work knowledge base in mental health and other areas of social work practice. The report included recommendations to NIMH and other federal agencies, professional associations in social work and social work education, social work education programs, and service agencies.

More than seven years have passed since the Task Force Report. During that period important developments have occurred in the effort to strengthen research resources within the field of social work. This chapter summarizes those developments and identifies areas of action that still need to be addressed. The chapter examines nationwide research resource developments against the background of the 1991 Task Force Report without attempting to examine the specific characteristics of individual research initiatives. It focuses on nationally visible research developments intended to contribute to the general body of knowledge used by social work practitioners and by other human service specialists. Social workers are involved in many other types of research that are not reflected in this report, including internal agency administrative and program studies, studies carried out as part of classroom instruction in social work education programs, and contract evaluation studies of individual service programs. Moreover, such research studies are only one part of the scholarly enterprise in which social work practitioners and social work educators regularly engage.

Significance of Social Work Research

In appointing the Task Force on Social Work Research in 1988 NIMH Director Dr. Lewis L. Judd said, ". . . we are entering an era when all modern and credible human and health service disciplines are increasingly seeing it as their fundamental responsibility to participate in advancing the knowledge bases of those scientific fields fundamental to their disciplines" (Task Force Report, 1991).

Social work practitioners are directly involved with some of the most critical human problems in today's society. The research initiatives that have developed during the 1990s directly address many of those problems, including the development, safety, and well-being of children and adolescents; mental illness; persistent household poverty; substance abuse; acute and chronic illness, including HIV-AIDS; problem conditions particularly affecting women; problems associated with race and ethnicity; and problems associated with the processes of aging.

In the period since the 1991 Task Force Report, demand has intensified in all areas of human services for research-based practice guidelines and for evidence of the effectiveness of service interventions. Some of the demand for cost-effectiveness evidence reflects pressures within managed health care and managed mental health care programs, which are among the largest employers of social work practitioners. Some of it reflects the demand for outcomes information from legislators and administrators as governmental funding organizations contract with other service organizations—public, nonprofit, and for-profit—to provide services to individuals, families, and communities. The development of replicable practice-relevant intervention studies has become increasingly important, both for individual social work practitioners and for the organized profession of social work.

Research Resource Developments

Research resource developments since the 1991 Task Force Report include investment by the National Institute of Mental Health; other national initiatives; developments in social work education programs; and research funding support.

INVESTMENT IN RESEARCH DEVELOPMENT BY THE NATIONAL INSTITUTE OF MENTAL HEALTH

"NIMH should provide support for research development in social work comparable to the support it has provided for research development in

Table 5.1. Social Work Research Development Centers

Center	Focus
George Warren Brown School of Social Work Washington University	Access to mental health care, integration of mental health services, and effectiveness of mental health care
The College of Social Work University of Tennessee	Organization and delivery of mental health services to children and adolescents
The School of Social Work University of Michigan	Poverty, risk, and mental health
The School of Social Work Portland State University	Organization and delivery of mental health care to children and adolescents
The School of Social Work University of Washington	Mental health, illness prevention services
The School of Social Work University of Pennsylvania	Care of persons with severe mental disorders
The School of Social Work University of Pittsburgh	Patient ecology, adherence, and treatment effectiveness

other mental health professions" (Task Force Report, 1991). The National Institute of Mental Health has responded to the 1991 Task Force Report in a very substantial manner. The National Institute of Mental Health has supported the establishment of research development centers, the creation of a national research support infrastructure, increased funding for research training and curriculum development, and increased support of individual competitive research proposals. These NIMH initiatives have been matched by a major effort by professional associations in social work and social work education programs to strengthen and expand research support structures and the body of practice-relevant research in social work.

Steven Hyman, MD, Director of the National Institute of Mental Health, stated in July 1996, "[as] people on the front-line of service, social workers can play a substantial role in studying the effectiveness of mental health care in real-world settings" (National Association of Social Workers, 1996).

Research Development Centers. The most dramatic proposal in the Task Force Report was the call for the creation of 10 Social Work Research Development Centers. In the period since the Task Force Report, seven Social Work Research Development Centers have been funded. Each center has received initial support for the development of research center infrastructure and the establishment of a multidisciplinary research development plan, as well as support for at least one major research project. The Research Development Centers and their major research foci are shown in Table 5.1.

By the end of 1997, proposals from 24 social work education programs for social work research development centers had been submitted to NIMH and reviewed by national research review committees. The assessment process has been rigorous and competitive, including multidisciplinary review panels consistent with the standards of the National Institutes of Health (NIH). A number of the funded centers have gone through several review cycles before final approval.

National Social Work Research Support Structure. In 1992 five professional organizations in social work—the Association of Baccalaureate Social Work Program Directors (BPD), National Association of Deans and Directors (NADD), Group for the Advancement of Doctoral Education (GADE), Council on Social Work Education (CSWE), and the National Association of Social Workers (NASW)—created the Institute for the Advancement of Social Work Research (IASWR). Established in office facilities provided by the National Association of Social Workers, IASWR was supported with funds from the five organizations. The Institute for the Advancement of Social Work Education received four years of support from NIMH to establish a national research resource center for the social work mental health field, to support the development of research training programs, and to provide technical assistance in the development of research proposals. The Institute for the Advancement of Social Work Research is currently supported by funding from the social work professional associations and project grants. The National Association of Social Workers has recently expanded the office space provided for the Institute.

The Institute for the Advancement of Social Work Research is governed by a board of directors appointed by the five participating organizations. An 11-member technical advisory committee also was established for IASWR in 1996. There have been three executive directors: Dr. Betsy Vourlekis (interim), Dr. Kathleen Ell, and Dr. John L. Lanigan, Jr. The Institute for the Advancement of Social Work Research has received consistent consultation and support from two members of NIMH professional staff, Dr. Juan Ramos and Dr. Kenneth Lutterman.

Research Training and Research Dissemination. The National Institute of Mental Health has provided support for a series of research training workshops and research institutes, and funded pre-doctoral and postdoctoral training grants in social work education programs. An extended research training workshop with 20 faculty participants was held at the University of Wisconsin in 1992–93. Research dissemination workshops were held annually between 1994 and 1998 at the University of Michigan, as follows:

· 1994—Child and Adolescent Mental Health Services Research
· 1995—Mental Health Epidemiology
· 1996—Intervention Research—PACT: Effective Community Treatment
· 1997—Intervention Research for Children and Adolescents: Multi-Systemic Family Treatment
· 1998—Poverty and Mental Health

A total of 135 participants attended these workshops. In 1997 in California, 80 social work faculty members and social work practitioners participated in four two-day research dissemination workshops. And, during the six years from 1992 to 1997, NIMH provided a number of pre-doctoral research training grants and two postdoctoral training grants. Individual grants also have been made to pre-doctoral and postdoctoral students in social work education programs. The Council on Social Work Education Minority Fellowship Program received funds from NIMH during these years for 20 students each year. In addition, undergraduate research trainee grants have been made during this period.

Faculty Research Development Awards. Although NIMH K-O8 Research Scientist Development Awards for Clinicians provide a major opportunity for junior faculty members in social work education programs to acquire the research expertise needed to establish a long-term program of research, no social work applications—and thus no awards—have been made.

Research Curriculum Development. The National Institute of Mental Health has supported the development of research curriculum guides and curriculum components. A grant from NIMH to the Group for the Advancement of Doctoral Education (GADE) resulted in the preparation of *Guidelines for Quality in Social Work Doctoral Programs* (1992). This report was distributed to the 55 graduate programs in social work that offer a doctoral degree in social work. A grant from NIMH to the Association of Baccalaureate Program Directors (BPD) resulted in the preparation of *Research and Undergraduate Social Work Education: A Report to the Profession* (1995). In the summer of 1997 an "Intensive Bachelor of Social Work Faculty Development Workshop, Focusing on Mental Health Research for Generalist Social Work" was held at Cornell University. The workshop's focus was the development of research curriculum modules for BSW programs with publication in the *Journal of Baccalaureate Social Work.* In 1998 a second research curriculum workshop was held for faculty members in BSW programs. Forty faculty members participated in these workshops. Research curriculum modules for doctoral programs have been prepared through a GADE program coordinated by Dr. James Moran. In 1998, at the request of CSWE and NADD, an MSW research curriculum development workshop was held with 20 faculty participants at Syracuse University.

Technical Assistance. The National Institute of Mental Health has provided technical assistance to individual researchers through NIMH staff members and through the contract between NIMH and IASWR. Technical assistance conferences have been held by the Director of IASWR and NIMH staff members in connection with the annual program meeting of the Council on Social Work Education (CSWE), NASW annual professional conference, and other social work conferences. In 1995 and 1997, one-day workshops on research proposal development included 25 social work faculty members. In 1997 and 1998, one-day workshops on dissertation grant proposal development included 52 doctoral students.

Research Support. In fiscal year (FY) 1993 NIMH made 38 research awards, totaling $9.5 million, to social work education programs or principal investigators with social work degrees. In FY 1995 there were 54 awards for $15.4 million, and in FY 97 there were 60. In FY 1993 there were five new or competing research awards to faculty and students in social work education programs; in FY 1995 there were 14 such awards, and in FY 97 there were 23.

During FY 1997, the most recent federal funding period, NIMH made six new and competing RO1 research grants; two R29 new investigator awards; seven small grants (including three dissertation research grants); three research enhancement projects at social work research development centers; and two research training grants. Altogether (including research training grants) grants from NIMH in FY 97 totaled some $15,000,000.

SUMMARY OF NIMH INVOLVEMENT

Since 1991, and guided by the Task Force recommendations, NIMH has provided major support for the development of mental health research resources within the professional field of social work. There has been a continuous and effective working relationship with national leadership associations in social work, individually and through IASWR, as well as with a large number of individual social work education programs. Funding for practice-relevant research has increased, both through the social work research development centers and through grants to individual researchers. Most importantly, NIMH has continually emphasized the importance of the development of high quality social work research for the provision of effective mental health services to individuals, families, and communities by social work practitioners and by other mental health professionals.

OTHER NATIONAL RESEARCH DEVELOPMENT INITIATIVES

"Research development requires concerted action by the major associations in social work and social work education" (Task Force Report, 1991). In addition to the initiatives supported through NIMH, other national research resource developments have been initiated through the organized profession of social work.

National Social Work Research Infrastructure. Each of the five participating professional associations has provided funding support for a total amount of $160,000 a year for IASWR over the past six years. In 1997 the Ford Foundation made a grant of $300,000 for support of IASWR over two years, replacing the funding support initially provided by NIMH. In 1997 IASWR was awarded a cooperative agreement by the Centers for Disease Control (CDC) for $1.6 million to coordinate the support of a four-year, three-site study of social work primary health care interventions. This project will involve collaboration with three social work education programs in carrying out the onsite research.

Table 5.2. Participation of Social Work Researchers in National Research Development Initiatives, 1991–1998

- Establishment of the Office of Behavioral and Social Science Research within the National Institutes of Health (NIH).
- Preparation of the report, *Enhancing Social Work Research on Military Women's Health* with funding from the Defense Women's Health Research Program (Department of Defense) (Ell & Martin, 1996).
- Organization of the Trans-NIH Symposium on Psychosocial Intervention: Social Work's Contribution (1996).
- Preparation of a report from the Ad Hoc Committee on Prevention Research in Social Work (1997) for the Work Group on Mental Disorders Prevention Research of the National Advisory Mental Health Council, National Institute of Mental Health.
- Participation through International Association of Social Work Researchers and the National Association of Social Workers in the establishment of the NIH Working Group on Child Abuse and Neglect (1997), involving five NIH Institutes, to develop a research agenda related to child abuse and neglect. In 1997 NIH released the report of the working group, *NIH Research on Child Abuse and Neglect: Current Status and Future Plans.* An NIH training workshop for child welfare researchers was held in 1998.
- Participation in the development of the United States Air Force Family Advocacy Program postdoctoral program at the School of Social Work, University of Maryland at Baltimore.
- Participation in the organization of a technical assistance seminar and workshop on substance abuse research, supported by the National Institute of Drug Abuse (1997).

In 1994 researchers in social work created the Society for Social Work and Research (SSWR). In 1998 SSWR had some 600 individual members. The first national conference of SSWR, co-sponsored by IASWR and with funding support from NIMH, was held in 1995. The second national conference of SSWR was held in January 1998, with a program that included the presentation of some 80 research papers. The third SSWR Conference was held in January 1999, and conferences are now to be held annually. The Quantitative Methods Interest Group (QMIG), which has met since 1989 in connection with the CSWE annual program meeting, has provided a forum for the exchange of information among faculty members teaching research methodology.

The Task Force on Administrative Research Infrastructures within Social Work Programs, created by NADD, prepared a report, *Challenges and Opportunities for Promoting Federally Funded Research in Social Work Programs* (1997). A workshop on "Developing Research Infrastructure in Social Work Schools/ Programs" was held at the George Warren Brown School of Social Work, Washington University, in October 1996, with co-sponsorship by IASWR and NIMH. Seventeen schools were represented. A summary report from the workshop was issued in 1997. "Building Research Infrastructure Among Social Work Programs," a leadership development institute cosponsored by IASWR and NADD, was held at the 1997 biannual meeting of NADD.

Research Development Initiatives. Through IASWR, members of the profession have participated in a series of national research development initiatives (listed in Table 5.2).

Research Dissemination. Opportunities for research dissemination within the profession have expanded. Three specialized social work research journals have been established since 1991: *Research on Social Work Practice* (Sage Publications); *Social Work Research* (NASW); and *The Journal of Social Work Research and Evaluation: An International Publication* (Springer Publishing Company). A review of existing social work research on mental health, *Advances in mental health research: Implications for practice* (Williams & Ell, 1998), was published by NASW.

The Society for Social Work and Research conferences have become a major opportunity for the presentation of significant research findings. However, as the audience is largely composed of research specialists, no established channel exists for bringing the results of these conferences systematically to the attention of the professional practitioner community.

Specialized national conferences also have taken place in the 1990s on research-related subjects. "Knowledge for Practice: Practitioners and Researchers as Partners" and a "National Symposium on Outcomes Measurement in the Human Services" were held at the Center for the Study of Social Work Practice, Columbia University School of Social Work, in November of 1993 and November of 1995, respectively. And a "National Conference on Research and Services in Support of Children and Their Families" was held at the Research and Training Center on Family Support and Children's Mental Health, Graduate School of Social Work, Portland State University, in May of 1997. Social work researchers also participate in many specialized national and international cross-disciplinary or multidisciplinary research conferences.

The annual conferences of NASW and CSWE are the largest gatherings of social work practitioners and social work educators. The planning of these conferences now reflects an increased awareness of the significance of knowledge-building research. For example, the CSWE call for papers now includes a specific empirical research category and NASW now involves IASWR in the development of research meetings for NASW annual conference. However, neither organization has made the annual conference a major showcase for significant knowledge-building and practice-relevant research.

SOCIAL WORK RESEARCH RESOURCE DEVELOPMENT IN SOCIAL WORK EDUCATION PROGRAMS

"Social work education programs are responsible for strengthening research education and research development" (Task Force Report, 1991). The information in this section came from the following sources:

· a 1995 NADD survey of social work education programs
· a 1997 e-mail inquiry to the members of SSWR
· a 1997 inquiry to deans and directors of social work education programs
· NIMH
· IASWR
· CSWE statistical reports

Research Development in Social Work Education Programs. In 1991 the Task Force on Social Work Research reported that some 10 to 12 social work education programs had either (1) organized programs of research with a formal research support infrastructure, or (2) a significant cadre of individual researchers (five or more) with nationally funded research projects. As of this writing, 16 social work education programs fit this description, including the seven programs with an NIMH Social Work Research Development Center grant. All of these social work education programs include doctoral education programs. In 1991 an additional 10 to 15 schools had the beginnings of an organized research infrastructure or at least two nationally funded researchers. Thirteen schools are in this category. These social work education programs also have doctoral education programs.

Thus some 29 social work education programs have sustained research development, including nationally funded research, in comparison with some 25 programs in 1991. In addition, another 25 social work education programs have at least one nationally funded researcher. Some of these programs have other very substantial research activities, including program evaluation studies, with state and local funding (both governmental and nongovernmental). More than 200 scholar-researchers receive some form of national funding—governmental and foundation—in some 55 social work education programs. Other active researchers, with funding support from state and local sources or from internal university sources, also engage in personal research as part of their academic activities.

Research Domains. An examination of the reports of ongoing research in social work education programs (including research centers and institutes) and the activities of individual funded researchers indicates a clustering of current research in several areas (listed in Table 5.3). These are not separate and discrete research domains; many of the topics overlap. Moreover, research addressed to issues of race and ethnicity is a focus that cuts across all of the above areas. Individual researchers may be involved with more than one of these subjects, and individual researchers in each of these domains are widely scattered. It is unclear that an ongoing community of social work researchers yet exists in any of these areas, although many of the researchers may be part of multidisciplinary communities of interest (for example, in the areas of substance abuse and gerontology). Also, a large number of scholar-researchers have indicated that they are interested in research dealing with social work practice generally, as well as research dealing with the nature of social work education, topics that, in some instances, overlap with the substantive research areas identified in Table 5.3.

Doctoral Education in Social Work. Doctoral programs in social work are the major resource for the preparation of researchers in social work, although a number of social work researchers receive advanced training in research through social science disciplines. However, over a period of nearly two decades little has changed in the number of doctoral graduates. Moreover,

substantial numbers of these doctoral graduates pursue advanced professional practice careers, or become faculty members in social work education programs that do not have a research support infrastructure. Given the
current wave of retirements among persons with research interests who
obtained doctorates in the 1950s and 1960s, it appears likely that current
doctoral programs are not contributing significantly to an expansion of the
total number of active scholar-researchers in social work.

The 1991 Task Force Report pointed out that the majority of doctoral
students enter doctoral education programs in their mid-30s after complet-
ing an MSW degree and an initial period of professional experience. These
doctoral students are, therefore, older than graduate students in most
academic fields, experience extended careers as doctoral students with only
a limited period of full-time study, and (in general) begin academic and
research careers in their early 40s. There is no indication that this pattern
has changed since 1991.

The number of doctoral programs in social work has increased slightly,
from 53 programs in 1992 to 56 programs in 1996. The number of doctoral
graduates has remained quite stable over an extended period, with 226 in
1980–81, 243 in 1991–92, 294 in 1993–94, and 258 in 1995–96. Since 1981
the annual number of reported doctoral graduates has varied from a low of
181 (1984–85) to a high of 332 (1987–88). In only one year (1987–88) has
the number of doctoral graduates risen above 300. (For comparison, the
number of MSW graduates grew from 9,750 to 14,484 during the same
period). The average number of doctoral graduates across all programs
during the 1990s has been 4.5 graduates per program, per year. In comparison, the programs have experienced an average of 8.5 admissions per year,
suggesting a 60 percent completion rate. Among recent doctoral students
(1996–97), 70 percent were women; and among recent doctoral graduates
(1996) 70 percent also were women. In 1992, 19.3 percent of doctoral
graduates were from African American, Latino, Native American, or Asian
American backgrounds; and in 1996, 16.3 percent of doctoral graduates
were from such backgrounds. A 1997 survey of doctoral programs indicated
that 27 percent of current doctoral students were from such backgrounds,
while the most recent CSWE report indicated that some 23 percent were
from such backgrounds.

RESEARCH FUNDING SUPPORT

"Support for research training and research development should also
come from federal agencies other than NIMH that are responsible for
service programs in fields of social work practice" (Task Force Report,
1991).

The National Institute of Drug Abuse (NIDA) has participated in discussions with IASWR about the establishment of a research development

Table 5.3. Social Work Research Domains and Examples

Domain	Example
Families, children, adolescents, child welfare, child abuse (300)	· Teenage parenting · Children with drug exposure · Children's exposure to violence · Mental health of children · Child abuse · Children in residential treatment and therapeutic foster care · Health and illness conditions among children · Kin and non-kin foster care · Open adoptions · Community-based services and the prevention of child abuse · Family preservation services · Permanency planning for abused children · Healthy Start programs · False reports of child abuse · Grief in childhood · Poverty, depression, and child health · HIV prevention and life options for youth in foster care
Mental health, mental illness (100)	· Community-based mental health services · Pre-adolescent suicidality · Child and adolescent diagnosis · Psycho-education and maintenance of community living · Children's exposure to violence and mental health · Organization and financing of mental health services · Mental health help seeking by African Americans and Caucasian Americans · Peer-support groups and mental illness · Use of mental health services by children in state custody · Mental health services for older adults · Access to mental health services · Effectiveness of mental illness treatment services · Costs of public mental health services
Health and illness (100)	· Women's health issues · Economic and political influences on state health policy · Managed health care and Medicaid · Hypertension in older adults · Impact of nutrition education programs in congregate meal sites · Prostate cancer prevention · Child/teen health program · Children's health · Children with HIV-AIDS · Occupational health hazards · HIV-AIDS and substance abuse · AIDS-related street out-reach

Table 5.3. Social Work Research Domains and Examples

Domain	Example
Gerontology and Aging (60)	· Evaluation and planning of services for older adults · Alzheimer's Disease · Aging processes · Quality assurance in long-term care · Social support among elderly · Caregiving for community-dwelling frail elderly · Interdisciplinary geriatric team training
Poverty/income maintenance/ social policy (60)	· Poverty law · Welfare reform · Employment training programs · Poverty and violence · Poverty and mental health · Supplemental Security Income and mental health policy · General assistance · Child support
Issues affecting Women (60)	· Women criminal offenders · Women and HIV-AIDS · Grandmothers raising children · Mental health and mental illness among women · Birth mothers and adoptive mothers · Women and substance abuse · Domestic violence and survivors · Women and homelessness · Adolescent mothers
Substance Abuse (40)	· Homelessness and substance abuse · Services for drug-abusing women and drug exposed children · Substance abuse treatment for individuals with HIV-AIDS · Motivational counseling for detoxification patients · Prevention of substance abuse

NOTE: Numbers in parentheses indicate the approximate number of social work researchers who identified that domain as an area of research interest.

program similar to the initiatives supported by NIMH. Currently no other federal agencies have considered a national strategy for research development in social work.

A wide variety of national sources are identified as providing research project funding by at least one social work education program. These include federal agencies and organizations and also national foundations. Members of the SSWR reported in 1997 that 46 percent of their funding for research came from federal sources and 37 percent came from private foundations (*SSWR News,* 1997).

At present, no systematic information exists about the level of research funding support across all social work education programs. However, some of the sources of research funding reported by social work education programs and individual researchers appear in Table 5.4.

Table 5.4. Funding Sources of Social Work Research Reported by Social Work Education Programs and Researchers

Federal	· National Institute of Mental Health
	· National Institute of Drug Abuse
	· National Institute for Nursing Research
	· National Institute of Aging
	· National Cancer Institute
	· National Institute of Alcohol and Alcohol Abuse
	· National Institute of Child Health and Human Development
	· National Institute of Allergy and Infectious Diseases
	· National Institute of Disability and Rehabilitation Research
	· National Institute of Dental Research
	· Administration for Children and Families
	· National Center of Child Abuse and Neglect
	· Assistant Secretary for Policy and Evaluation
	· Office of Human Development Services
	· Children's Bureau
	· Center for Social Services Research
	· Administration on Aging
	· Centers for Disease Control
	· Center for Mental Health Policy and Services Research
	· Office of Substance Abuse Prevention
	· Health Care Financing Administration
	· Medicaid
	· U.S. Department of Justice
	· Bureau of Justice Assistance, National Institute of Justice
	· National Institute on Juvenile Justice and Delinquency
	· U.S. Department of Education
	· U.S. Department of Housing and Urban Development
	· National Academy of Science
	· National Science Foundation
	· Veterans Administration
National foundations	· Milbank
	· W.K. Kellogg Foundation
	· George Gund Foundation
	· Ewing Marion Kauffman Foundation
	· Aspen Institute
	· Rockefeller Foundation
	· Edna McConnell Clark Foundation
	· John A. Hartford Foundation
	· Pfizer Foundation

Current sources for the support of research reported by social work education programs also include state and local governments, state and local foundations, and private corporations.

Significant efforts are being made to expand the base of support for social work research among federal research organizations. However, no national-level approach exists to strengthen the base of support for social work research among major national foundations, many of which are concerned with the social conditions that also engage social work researchers.

SUMMARY OF CURRENT RESEARCH RESOURCE DEVELOPMENTS

Substantial expansion of research resources within the organized profession of social work has occurred since the 1991 Task Force Report, primarily in connection with social work education programs. The response of NIMH to the report has been very significant, given the wide range of research commitments facing the Institute. The National Institute of Mental Health has supported the development of a national infrastructure for research development, funded Social Work Research Development Centers, and supported improvements in research training. In addition, the number of social work researchers receiving competitive research funding has increased. The Institute for the Advancement of Social Work Research has established an important precedent of collaboration among the four professional education associations and NASW in pursuit of common goals. Future development of research resources within social work will depend heavily on the continuation of that collaboration.

Primarily through IASWR, the profession of social work has participated in developments in fields beyond mental health (including the NIH Working Group on Child Abuse and Neglect and the National Institute on Drug Abuse) that may broaden the support base for social work research development. Other significant developments at the national level included the creation of the Society for Social Work and Research (SSWR). Potential sources within social work for dissemination of knowledge-building research findings to the practitioner community, and to the community-at-large, have increased. However, it is unclear that the desired dissemination and communication with the current practice community are actually taking place.

The challenge of competing for a Social Work Research Development Center grant—or even the consideration of developing an application for such a grant—has strengthened research infrastructures within individual social work education programs and increased the number of social work education programs with an organized research infrastructure. Systematic attention to strengthening research education has taken place throughout the professional curriculum, including BSW, MSW, and doctoral programs. An important series of research training workshops and technical assistance institutes have taken place for faculty members in social work education programs.

However, little change is apparent in the scope of specialized research training across social work education programs. The number of doctoral graduates remains essentially static, and very limited use has been made of postdoctoral research training opportunities. In part this reflects the high demand for teaching faculty with doctoral qualifications as enrollments in existing social work education programs expand and as new programs are established.

Those social work education programs with a strong commitment to research are drawing support for individual research initiatives from a wide variety of national funding sources, both governmental and nongovernmental. However, to date, NIMH is the only source that has provided broad-based funding support for research resource development in social work.

The resources devoted to research development in social work have increased markedly. There has been a substantial increase in the attention given to research development by national leaders within the profession, and within individual social work education programs. The development of research resources, more than any other aspect of professional development, requires national level initiatives. The primary funding sources for knowledge-building, practice-relevant research are at the national level—federal research agencies and national foundations. The continued development of research resources within social work requires collaborative relationships with federal agencies in addition to NIMH, with national organizations in other human service professions, and with leadership foundations.

Much of the attention in this progress report has focused on specific developments that have taken place in social work professional education programs. It is essential, however, to remember that the purpose for expanding research resources is to improve the quality of the services provided by the several hundred thousand practicing social workers who work directly with children, families and communities.

Issues for the Future

The first section of this chapter described specific developments that have taken place since 1991. It also pointed to critical issues that continue to require attention from members of the organized profession, including both practicing professionals and participants in social work education programs. The following discussion emphasizes the need to strengthen the contributions social work research can make to the development of the practicing profession, rather than to the career advancement of individual researchers or the improvement of the relative status of social work education programs within academic communities (although these are also relevant objectives).

During the 1990s practice-relevant research for social work practitioners has become a crucial issue in professional survival. Demands come from all directions for research-based practice guidelines and for evidence of professional effectiveness, including agency-based practice and practice in the world of managed health care and managed behavioral health care. Almost equally important are demands for evidence that professional interventions are not actively harmful. Research on the effectiveness of service interventions is a major form of representation of the profession to the larger society. The most important issue for the immediate future is to bring the practice effectiveness concerns of social work practitioners together with the resources represented by social work researchers.

RESEARCH DEVELOPMENT

The current pattern of research activities includes great diversity and involves a substantial number of individual researchers in individual studies. However, it is crucial to distinguish between studies that are interesting, career-building intellectual activities or responses to local funding opportunities and studies that address a central professional practice issue. The former type of study often results only in an unpublished report to a funder or a single journal article, whereas the latter type, through broader publication, becomes part of a cumulative knowledge-building process. In particular, well-conceptualized, well-designed, replicable studies of practice interventions are part of a larger knowledge-building process that justifies systematic and substantial support, both from within the organized profession and from national funding sources.

The *Summary Report of the Workshop on Developing Research Infrastructure in Social Work Schools/Programs* (1997) and the *National Association of Deans and Directors Report* (1997) identified critical elements in establishing a sustained, knowledge-building research endeavor in social work education programs. These elements are listed in Table 5.5. The initial Social Work Research Development Center at the George Warren Brown School of Social Work, Washington University, provides an example of how a variety of resources can be combined for sustained research development. Among the potentially important resources for research development in social work are the KO-8 Research Scientist Development Awards for Clinicians. However, there have been no NIMH applications from researchers in social work education programs for these opportunities.

DOCTORAL EDUCATION

The period since the 1991 Task Force Report has brought little change in the development of new research scholars through doctoral and postdoctoral studies. While the number of doctoral programs has increased, the number of doctoral graduates has not changed significantly. Neither has the level of postdoctoral research training opportunities, there being only two schools with NIMH institutional funding for postdoctoral students. Among social work doctoral education programs, only two-thirds define their primary objective as the preparation of scholar-researchers. The remaining one-third define their primary objective as the preparation of advanced practitioners. The proportion of women among doctoral graduates and among doctoral students has remained relatively constant at 70

Table 5.5. Critical Elements in Establishing Sustained Research in Social Work Education Programs

- Leadership by the academic dean or director in research development
- Strengthening of research training in doctoral programs and active involvement of doctoral students in ongoing research initiatives
- Development of post-doctoral research training opportunities
- Collaboration among the practice community and human service agencies
- Establishment of a research culture that stresses the importance of research in all aspects of the social work education program and that creates public visibility for research
- Establishment of a research culture that stresses interactions among research, teaching, and service activities
- A core of seasoned researchers
- Establishment of non-tenure research positions that receive equal recognition with tenure-track positions in the academic community
- Development of a research team model that includes interdisciplinary participation rather than relying primarily on a solo researcher model
- Completion of pilot studies and publication of research data and analysis from pilot studies
- Use of an internal peer-review process before proposals are submitted to external funding sources
- Strengthening of the role of research mentors and greater connection of junior researchers with senior researchers
- Collaboration among social work researchers in free-standing research institutes or centers and involving multiple social work education programs
- Provision of technical and administrative support for research

NOTE: Adapted from *Summary Report: A Workshop on Developing Research Infrastructure in Social Work Schools/Programs* (Washington University, 1997) and National Association of Deans and Directors Report (1997).

percent. The proportion of doctoral graduates who come from African American, Latino, American Indian, and Asian American backgrounds has decreased, although a recent survey of PhD programs suggests that some 25 percent of current students are from such backgrounds.

Social work doctoral education programs continue to face the problem of recruiting social workers with practice experience as doctoral students while providing very limited financial support. Limitations in financial support may contribute to the gap between the proportion of doctoral students from Latino, African American, American Indian, and Asian American backgrounds (25 percent) and the proportion of such individuals among doctoral graduates (16 percent).

The practice experience expectation for doctoral students is reinforced by the CSWE accreditation requirement of two years' practice experience for faculty members who are to teach professional practice methods. This requirement limits the opportunity for MSW graduates with a strong research interest, regardless of the amount of their pre-MSW practice experience, to pursue doctoral studies in social work immediately following the completion of MSW studies.

The requirement may, in general, have positive implications for the quality of teaching in professional degree programs. However, it has not been matched by appropriate levels of financial support for doctoral students who do bring practice experience. This has had the effect of largely precluding participation in doctoral studies by many individuals with successful practice careers, individuals with substantial household financial responsibilities, and individuals who have large educational loan burdens at the end of their MSW education. Moreover, the limitations on financial assistance encourage extended, part-time programs of study, which are not consistent with the development of well-qualified research scholars. Critical decisions on doctoral support levels will have to be made within individual social work education programs, even if some modest increase in support from governmental sources could be obtained for doctoral and postdoctoral students in particular fields of research.

The author recommends that financial support for doctoral students who are preparing for careers as scholar-researchers be substantially increased in both level and duration through action by individual schools of social work, and that this issue be given high priority by the National Association of Deans and Directors of Schools of Social Work and the Group for the Advancement of Doctoral Education in Social Work.

DISSEMINATION

It is unclear that systematic dissemination of research-based information to the practitioner community is actually happening, although the opportunities for research dissemination have increased since the 1991 Task Force Report. Both CSWE and NASW give some attention to research-based presentations at national conferences, but such presentations have not been a priority, as reflected in major, invitational all-conference presentations. The publication programs of both NASW and CSWE potentially provide a critical resource to the extent that they deal specifically with practice-relevant research. A major issue in providing knowledge-building research and information to the practice community through peer-reviewed journals has to do with access to cross-disciplinary research for which a social work researcher is not the principal investigator or lead author. A second, persistent issue, involves the question of whether general professional journals in social work, as in other professional fields, are intended to serve primarily as publication outlets for the diverse interests of members of the academic faculty, or as consistent sources of tested information for the practitioner community. It may be that cross-disciplinary research journals with a specialized focus in a specific practice domain are more relevant for both researchers and practitioners than multitopic journals limited to a single professional or academic discipline.

Social workers need to explore ways in which contemporary forms of communication, including the Internet and the World Wide Web, can be used to develop a community of researchers in particular domains as well as to make the results of research accessible to individual practitioners. The information available through such networks should include developments in other professions as well as in social work.

The author recommends that CSWE and NASW establish the priority of research-based, practice-relevant presentations at annual conferences, including invitational, all-conference presentations; that the publication policies of NASW be reviewed to determine the specific relevance of its publications to the social work practice community, and to examine the potential inclusion of research-based knowledge from other professions and disciplines in such publications; and that CSWE and NASW provide leadership in exploring the potential contribution of creating electronic channels for information-sharing networks in relevant social work research domains.

RESEARCH DEVELOPMENT DOMAINS

Research dealing with issues related to problematic conditions affecting children, adolescents, families with children, and the child welfare system, and research dealing with mental health and mental illness, are, at the moment, the most substantial domains of research development in social work. Many current studies in these two domains also cross-cut other issues of research interest, including issues involving women and issues involving race and ethnicity. The presentations at the 1998 SSWR annual conference were consistent with this pattern. Research reports dealing with mental health issues and issues affecting children, adolescents, and child welfare accounted for 50 percent of the presentations. Another one-third dealt with health issues, including HIV-AIDS; substance abuse; and health issues affecting women; and 10 percent of the presentations dealt explicitly with race, ethnicity or cultural competence issues. The balance dealt primarily with issues in research methodology. Each of the major social work research domains reflected in the current pattern of research initiatives among social work researchers involves different opportunities and constraints.

Mental Health. Mental health research is marked by the existence of a major federal agency, NIMH, with a long history of research funding. A large mental health research establishment is supported by funding from pharmaceutical firms as well as by governmental and foundation sources. The National Institute of Mental Health has been the major source of increased institutional support for research development in social work since 1991, as well as a source of support for many years before that for the development of professional education in social work. However, a number of critical issues are involved in the future of support for mental health and mental illness research in social work.

The institutional context of mental health services is changing dramatically, and so is the nature of critical research questions. First, the use of medications to control biologically based forms of mental illness will continue to expand. This may mean less attention will be paid to psychosocial interventions to prevent serious and chronic mental illness, such as schizophrenia, and much more attention will be paid to psychosocial interventions to support ongoing treatment of a chronic illness condition.

Second, in the near future the provision of publicly funded mental health services, including Medicaid-supported services, will be largely privatized, including "managed behavioral health care" contracts with health maintenance organizations. Even the operation of what have been inpatient public psychiatric hospitals is often contracted to for-profit hospital firms or to medical schools. Indeed, most acute mental health services, regardless of the source of funding, may be largely folded into insurance-based, privately managed general health care systems. Researchers dealing with mental health patients will have to develop working relationships with for-profit behavioral health care firms and establish research objectives that can contribute to the effectiveness of services provided by such firms.

Beginning in 1998 the question of renewing or extending the infrastructure support of the initial social work research development centers arose. Continuation of support for research infrastructure in existing centers may compete with funds for additional research development centers. However, a sustained effort to establish additional research development centers is warranted. These centers have proved to be a very effective method of stimulating and encouraging the development of multidisciplinary research infrastructures. Applications for extended support of current research development centers will require serious examination of the results from the initial funding. Specifically, this will involve consideration of how many research proposals have been funded and, equally important, what results from the initial studies have contributed to the knowledge base of social work practice in mental health. The National Institute for Mental Health has announced a general program for funding Specialized Mental Health Intervention Research Centers. Serious attention might be given by existing Social Work Research Development Centers, or other programs with an established research infrastructure, to submitting proposals under this program.

It is important to determine which findings about intervention methods are relevant for systematic presentation to the field of social work. This process has begun with the publication of *Advances in mental health research: Implications for practice* (Williams & Ell, 1998). Peer testing of findings and research replication are essential.

The author recommends that the Social Work Research Development Centers lead the assessment of the existing body of social work research dealing with mental health and mental illness to determine those findings that are substantial enough to test in multisite studies. In turn, effective communication of such findings must be made to the current practice community, as well as to other professional disciplines.

Services for Children, Adolescents, and Families, and Child Abuse or Child Welfare Services. Child welfare and child protective services, and residential services for children, constitute the most distinctively social work sector of professional practice. Child welfare and child abuse services, particularly the public services, also exist in a state of almost total crisis. A 1997 Government Accounting Office (GAO) report begins by saying, "The CPS [Child Protective Service] system is in crisis, plagued by difficult problems, such as growing caseloads, increasingly complex social problems underlying child maltreatment, and ongoing systemic weaknesses in day-to-day operations." The report identifies several "new strategies" that were identified in a study of four states, but it then adds, ". . . there is little or no research to assess whether these new strategies effectively solve the problems of abused and neglected children and their families."

To a large degree the future credibility of social work as a profession in the public sector is tied to the public child welfare and child protective services system. The credibility of social work in child welfare depends substantially on the ability of social work to identify research-based interventions that are relevant to the problems faced by the CPS system. Participation by schools of social work in the in-service training of CPS workers, funding for which has been increased in the last federal budget, is of limited relevance if the training is built around service models that are in a state of collapse. National attention has been focused on these issues with the passage of the Adoption and Safe Families Act of 1997. This legislation represented, in part, an effort by Congress to micromanage state-administered systems that have not been functioning effectively.

Unlike mental health, child welfare research has no clearly focused institutional support system. While there has been support for individual research initiatives through the National Center on Child Abuse and Neglect and the Children's Bureau, these agencies have no national research strategy. As the GAO report states, "The members of our expert panel believe the federal research agenda is too broad. . . . [T]he major research questions that are relevant to [state] CPS units are inadequately addressed because the total amount of funds authorized for research is low and spread among too many other projects." The NIH Task Force on Child Abuse and Neglect brought together five NIH Institutes, with leadership by NIMH. But none of the Institutes has this as a central, or priority, research issue, even though NIMH is the major source of funding for research dealing with child and adolescent mental health issues. The NIH Child Abuse and Neglect Work Group (1997) reported:

> Given the array of obstacles that have hampered research efforts in the child maltreatment area to date, isolated efforts addressing any single problem area are not likely to be successful. Instead, a coordinated, concerted effort to address the range of infrastruc-

tural, content-related and translational problems will be needed to generate and maintain the necessary research progress to address this important health problem in children and families. (p. 21)

Child welfare research lacks a substantial interdisciplinary research framework, in contrast to mental health research. Few research colleagues in other academic departments are likely to view child welfare as their primary research area. Child welfare research also involves some of the most difficult obstacles in developing research collaboration with existing service organizations, as identified in the report of the NIH Child Abuse and Neglect Working Group (1997). Progress in child welfare research requires establishing a national research support framework, including both federal agencies and national foundations, as well as national child welfare associations such as the National Association of Public Child Welfare Administrators (NAPCWA) and the Child Welfare League of America (CWLA). It also requires establishing a consensus about what we already know from current research, for example, research dealing with family support, family preservation and community-based response systems, and creating a future research agenda.

If social work fails to provide research leadership in child welfare, a serious knowledge-building program of intervention research may not ever develop (in contrast to a repeated series of descriptive and explanatory studies documenting the characteristics of child abuse and of system problems). As a society, we could drift toward a public child protective services system that deals with only the most extreme situations and relies largely on the removal of children and criminal punishment of parents as the standard operating procedure.

The author recommends that a social work initiative be established in cooperation with relevant organizations within the U.S. Department of Health and Human Services to (1) assess existing research dealing with services that support families and communities, services that respond to child abuse and neglect, and the child welfare and child protective services systems; (2) develop a national research agenda; and (3) create the national resources required to support such an agenda.

Health and Illness. Social work research in health is part of a large, complex, and competitive multidisciplinary research field similar to mental health. Individual researchers are more likely to be part of interdisciplinary research networks than to be part of a distinctive social work health research network. Unlike mental health, the national funding structures for health and illness are spread across all of the National Institutes of Health as well as across many of the national foundations. This research area cuts across all age groups and all economic levels. It is a research area in which issues relevant to women and to persons from diverse ethnic and racial backgrounds are particularly important. Research development in social work health research likely will depend primarily on initiatives by a single researcher, or by a research team in a single social work institution collaborating with researchers in other fields and other disciplines. In addition to studies dealing with specific health conditions, increased social work participation in policy studies dealing with issues in the organization of managed health care and the provision of health care services is important. Policies affecting provision of health care will affect individuals and families who have been served by public health care programs in the past.

The author recommends that IASWR support the development of a network among researchers particularly interested in issues related to health and social work, for the purposes of information exchange, development of collaborative, multisite studies, and identification of relevant sources of research support.

Gerontology. Worldwide over the next several decades, the population of individuals over 65 years old and outside of the labor force will increase dramatically. User preferences, and improvements in personal health and in medical care, indicate a sharp increase in community-based service arrangements, and a need for research on the effectiveness of alternative service arrangements. Research on the long-term effects of caregiving on family caregivers also is needed. Moreover, the increase in the economic resources of many older adults, and their adult children, indicates that this is an area that may support both agency-based and marketplace services, a factor that should be considered in research development.

Like child welfare and services for children, gerontology is a major area of social work practice. The current Department of Health and Human Services assistant secretary for aging and the immediately preceding assistant secretary are both social workers. Gerontology also is a major interdisciplinary research area. However, social work has not yet established strong institutional connections with the major federal research institution, the National Institute on Aging.

The author recommends that IASWR, in cooperation with social work researchers in gerontology, initiate an exploration of potential opportunities for research collaboration involving the Office of the Assistant Secretary for Aging, the National Institute on Aging, the Administration on Aging, the Health Care Financing Administration, and the Social Security Administration.

Poverty and Income Assistance. Historically, poverty and income assistance have held a central policy focus in social work education. However, social work involvement in substantive research, other than historical research, generally has been limited to a few institutions where social work has been a partner in nationally recognized multidisciplinary research programs or a participant in international comparative policy studies. The limited involvement of social work researchers in this domain was reflected in the general absence of presentations dealing with such policy research in the 1998 SSWR conference. Poverty and welfare reform research requires collaboration with social science researchers in economics, political science, sociology, anthropology, history, and public policy, a pattern of collaboration that requires crossing disciplinary turf barriers. It also requires long-term, multisite studies to examine the full effects of these policy changes as well as intensive small-scale qualitative studies of particular sub-groups among the persons most directly affected.

The recent welfare reform transformation has widespread implications for social work practice, both at the direct services level and at the policy level. Moreover, a direct connection exists between welfare reform and changes in the organization and funding of health and mental health services (and the role of social workers in these programs). Developments in income assistance policy in the United States also may have implications for similar policies, and for social work practice, in other industrialized societies. These developments are also directly connected to concerns about the welfare of children and the public child welfare system. Yet, social work has very limited representation in the major national research initiatives to track the consequences of welfare reform or the consequences of the reorganization and privatization of public health and public mental health services. Although there are some federal and state research initiatives in these areas, the most important studies are large-scale, substantially funded initiatives by national foundations with the individual involvement of only a few social work researchers. Support of expanded social work research in these areas may require, in particular, approaching national foundations rather than federal agencies, as federal and state policies have already been established.

The author recommends that a consortium of social work research centers dealing with public policy issues and initiatives relating to poverty and welfare reform initiate discussions with national foundations and organizations involved with similar research efforts. The goal of the discussions would be to develop a plan for the contribution of social work research to future public policy discussions dealing with these issues. Moreover, the discussion should include an examination of the interface between public policies in income assistance and public policies in the provision of health care services.

Issues Affecting Women. Research dealing with problems affecting women is a central focus in studies of poverty and welfare reform and child abuse and neglect. In other areas such as health, mental health, corrections, and substance abuse, conditions specifically affecting women often have been overlooked until recently. Research on issues affecting women has become increasingly visible across the academic community, involving a large number of different disciplines and professional education programs. There is no single research funding source for which this is a primary focus, including psychosocial conditions as well as health conditions, although research on health conditions affecting women has been given a priority status in NIH. Social work has historically been concerned with social and economic problems affecting women, but often with a limited, specialized focus. Research dealing with economic conditions affecting women who are single parents is separated from research on the caregiving responsibilities of such women involving both children and parents. Research on the experience of women from one type of cultural background is separated from research on the experience of women from other backgrounds. Social work has an unusual opportunity to bring together research on the many factors affecting the experience of women in American society, including, but not limited to, women in very low income households. Even more important would be the development of studies of interventions that are designed specifically to deal with conditions that directly affect women.

The author recommends that IASWR support the development of a network among researchers particularly interested in issues directly affecting women for information exchange, for the development of collaborative, multisite studies, and for the identification of relevant sources of research support.

Substance Abuse. Substance abuse, including nicotine addiction, is linked with nearly every other social work concern—child abuse, family violence, mental illness, HIV-AIDS, health and illness, corrections, and adolescent development. It is a topic area with two major federal research funding sources, the National Institute of Drug Abuse and the National Institute of Alcoholism and Alcohol Abuse, as well as research support programs in the Substance Abuse and Mental Health Services Administration (SAMHSA). In this domain a substantial amount of biomedical research as well as psychological research is currently underway. But it remains a domain in which there are few conclusive answers, either about effective treatment or effective prevention. This is also a service domain that involves many practicing social workers. The development of more effective models of intervention is a very high priority. This is also a domain in which the development of a research network within social work and the establishment of a national research development strategy, with an emphasis on intervention research, should be a high priority. With new research support initiatives being developed by the National Institute for Drug Abuse, including a National Drug Treatment Clinical Trials Network, responses from the research institutions within social work become very important.

The author recommends that IASWR actively promote the continued development of new substantive social work research support initiatives in cooperation with the National Institute for Drug Abuse, with active support from each of the five IASWR participating organizations.

Summary. Each of these substantive research domains requires a different developmental strategy to strengthen the relevant research base in social work. Some domains primarily require continued research development leadership through IASWR. Others (child welfare, for example) require a national research strategy developed by the entire social work community. Some domains (health and HIV-AIDS, for example) primarily require research design initiatives by individual researchers and individual social work education programs in interdisciplinary fields with multiple funding sources. Others (such as poverty and welfare reform) require a combination of national initiatives and initiatives by individual research programs to establish working relationships with national foundations.

The author recommends that each of these domains needs the following: (1) an assessment of the state of knowledge from social work and related disciplines; (2) an identification of critical knowledge gaps; and (3) an identification of specific research needs, and of opportunities to fill these knowledge gaps.

Particularly important in the development of social work research in all of these domains is the continuous examination of the connections between poverty, race and ethnicity, and institutionalized discrimination, and the specific, substantive, practice-relevant questions being examined. There is also a need to bring information from research in these domains to bear on the professional practice issues faced by social work practitioners. A national summit on practice-relevant research is urgently needed to bring together leadership from the practice community in each of these domains through NASW, and research leadership from the social work professional education associations and the SSWR.

FUNDING

Funding issues involve the support of research development by the organized profession of social work and by national research centers. They also involve the development of strategies to obtain expanded, ongoing funding support for practice-relevant intervention research from both governmental and nongovernmental sources. The establishment by NIMH of the Social Work Research Development Center competitive grant program and the funding of seven social work research development centers has dramatically affected the development of mental health research resources within social work. It is critical that this grant program be continued, with an opportunity for new grant proposal submissions, together with the technical assistance services that have been essential to its current effectiveness. Similar support from other national research centers in critical areas of social work research is also essential for broadening the base of research development within social work.

The author recommends that NIMH continue its funding support of the Social Work Research Development Center program with opportunities for new grant proposal submissions, and that other national research centers, such as the National Institute of Drug Abuse and the National Institute of Aging, establish similar competitive grant programs.

The Institute for the Advancement of Social Work Education is a critical instrument for the entire field of social work if there is to be a long-term strategy for strengthening funding support for research resource development as well as for individual research projects. Financial support for IASWR must continue to be a high priority for each of the participating professional associations.

The author recommends that NASW, CSWE, BPD, NADD, and GADE continue to provide funding and institutional support for IASWR, and that they also seek permanent endowment expanded support for IASWR from foundations and individuals so that it can take on the leadership responsibilities recommended above.

The 1991 Task Force Report recommended that NASW establish "an Office to educate the profession about the importance of research to the future strength, advancement, creditability and influence of the profession" (p. 79). The task force also recommended that CSWE establish "an Office to promote and facilitate research education and research development within social work education" (p. 81). Further, CSWE has included the following recommendation in its strategic plan for 1998–2000:

> Goal 2. Promote all avenues for the development of knowledge relevant to social work education, practice, and policy; strengthen the research component of social work education; and pursue multiple means for timely, accessible knowledge dissemination (including the use of newer technologies). (CSWE, 1998, p. 15)

The author recommends that CSWE, consistent with the 1991 Task Force recommendations, establish a fully funded staff position in support of the integration of research-based, practice-relevant knowledge into the professional curriculum at all levels; and that NASW establish a fully funded staff position to support application of research-based, practice-relevant knowledge by the present body of professional practitioners.

The major external source of developmental funding for research in social work since 1991 has been NIMH. Establishment of a broader, more diverse base of funding support for research development in social work is a critical task. There have been initial discussions through IASWR with the National Institute on Drug Abuse about a program of support for research development relevant to its mission, with preliminary initiatives now underway.

It is of the highest priority that a strategy for financial support of a multi-institution program of social work research dealing with children and adolescents and with child welfare and child protective service programs be created. A precedent has been established with the multi-institution funding structures involved in child welfare training. Potentially, the development of such a program should involve the Office of the Secretary of Health and Human Services, the NIH Working Group on Child Abuse and Neglect, the National Center for Child Abuse and Neglect, and the Children's Bureau.

Social work researchers in individual social work education programs are being supported by a number of national foundations, as well as by many state and local foundations. However, it is essential to gain greater recognition by national foundations of the potential contributions of social work research to their research objectives. The development of a framework of expanded and sustained funding support for research—in particular, replicable intervention research—will require national leadership and national resources. The National Association of Social Workers and CSWE are the major national leadership centers for the profession.

The author recommends that NASW and CSWE, in cooperation with IASWR, develop a national strategy for developing a sustained funding base for practice-relevant, replicable intervention research in social work.

Conclusion

The position and status of the social work profession within American society are not controlled by the profession but instead largely determined by the perceptions of other individuals in other institutions. Both the process and the content of research in social work are major forms of communication and representation of social work to the broader society. Many important developments in social work research have occurred since 1991, primarily as a result of support through NIMH. But social work research also faces critical challenges. Urgent needs include the following:

· strengthening doctoral and postdoctoral research training programs
· developing a research strategy that is relevant to the challenges facing the entire field of child welfare and child protective services
· broadening the funding base for social work research through the involvement of additional federal research agencies and national foundations.

Among the social work education programs that have established a significant research infrastructure, the issue now is developing investigations of social work intervention initiatives. The study of social work interventions must, in turn, be directly connected with strengthening the processes through which the research results are disseminated to the practice community to help the individuals, families, and communities that social work serves. Only as research contributes systematically to the knowledge base and improves professional practice (in all of its forms) can there really be a justification for expanded financial support for such research.

Author's Note

This chapter is based on a presentation made at the Society for Social Work
and Research Conference in North Miami, Florida, in January 1998. The
initial presentation was a preliminary version of the *Report on Progress in the
Development of Research Resources in Social Work,* which was developed at the
initiative of the Institute for the Advancement of Social Work Research
(IASWR). The presentation was subsequently revised and sent to the Board
of IASWR in July 1998. This chapter is a version of that final report.

References

Association of Baccalaureate Social Work Program Directors. (1995). *Research and undergradu-
ate social work education.* Rochester, NY: Author.
Council on Social Work Education. (1998). Council on Social Work Education Strategic Plan:
1998–2000. *Social Work Education Reporter, 46 (1),* 15.
Ell, K. R., & Martin, J. A. (1996). *Enhancing social work research on military women's health.*
Washington, DC: Institute for the Advancement of Social Work Research.
Group for the Advancement of Doctoral Education in Social Work. (1992). *Guidelines for quality
in social work doctoral programs.* New Brunswick: Rutgers, the State University of New Jersey.
Government Accounting Office. (1997). *Child welfare: States' progress in implementing family
preservation and support services* (HEHS-97–34). Washington, DC: Author.
Institute for the Advancement of Social Work Research. (1997, September). *A workshop on
developing research infrastructure in social work schools/programs: Summary report.* Washington,
DC: Author.
Judd, L. L. (1988). Presentation at Columbus, Ohio (October 6). Austin: Archives of the
University of Texas at Austin, Task Force on Social Work Research.
National Institutes of Health. (1997). *NIH research on child abuse and neglect: Current status and
future plans.* Washington, DC: Author.
National Association of Deans and Directors of Schools of Social Work. (1997, April).
Challenges and opportunities for promoting federally funded research in social work programs.
Washington, DC: Author.
NIMH director: Front-line studies vital. (1996, September). *NASW News,* p. 13.
Society for Social Work and Research. (1997, February). *SSWR News.* New York: Author.
Task Force on Social Work Research. (1991). *Building social work knowledge for effective services
and policies: A plan for research development.* Austin: University of Texas at Austin School of
Social Work.
Williams, J., & Ell, K. (1998). *Advances in mental health research: Implications for practice.*
Washington, DC: National Association of Social Workers.

Conclusion

Miriam Potocky-Tripodi and Tony Tripodi

I n this conclusion we review the major themes of the preceding chapters and identify new directions for the future of social work practice research.

One recurrent theme, emphasized by Kahn, by Rosen, Proctor, and Staudt, by Kazi, and by Austin, has been the critical need for social work research to generate knowledge about what interventions work, for whom, and under what conditions. Clearly this need calls for more evaluative research in social work. All of the authors noted the importance of traditional program evaluation methodology, namely, the randomized clinical trial (RCT). However, most of the chapter authors also made it clear that such experiments must be placed within the context of practice and the existing continuum of knowledge in the relevant practice field.

Kazi described and advocated an approach to applied knowledge-building using the scientific realist paradigm. He placed evaluation research within a holistic research context that addresses "four key concerns for practitioners":

1. How to select a model of intervention
2. How to use effectiveness research in the selection process
3. How to target the intervention in pre-existing contexts
4. How to improve the intervention models based on evaluation research. (p. 73)

The essence of Kazi's developmental approach is embodied in his statement that "evaluation research is about improving the construction of [intervention] models, and therefore about improving the content of the practice itself" (p. 73). Rosen, Proctor, and Staudt emphasized that the purposes of knowledge need to be more clearly related to its functions in practice.

While most of the contributing authors called for these kinds of practice-relevant research activities, they also pointed sharply to the paucity of such studies in the profession's current body of scholarship. Most clearly made by Rosen, Proctor, and Staudt, this criticism was echoed by Kahn and Austin. All of these authors also acknowledged the difficulties of conducting such studies, and identified inadequate supportive infrastructures and funding as the major obstacles. Rosen, Proctor, and Staudt also speculated that social work researchers' socialization into the aims of social science (description, explanation, and prediction) may lead many to preclude applied research aims.

We are not so certain that these forces are more to blame than the "convenience factor" we mentioned in our introduction to this volume. Kahn observed that a social work researcher may "take his or her problem not from a strategic approach to knowledge-building but from locally and personally-defined priorities, or from what is at the moment attractive to public or private funding sources, or from priorities popular to topic-approving faculties in PhD programs. Such results are seldom additive" (p. 29). Similarly, Austin noted that "it is crucial to distinguish between studies that are interesting, career-building intellectual activities or responses to local funding opportunities and studies that address a central professional practice issue. The former type of study often results only in an unpublished report to a funder or a single journal article, whereas the latter type, through broader publication, becomes part of a cumulative knowledge-building process" (p. 106).

To use Rosen, Proctor, and Staudt's terminology, it seems that many social work researchers have been "socialized" into doing research that is convenient or personally interesting but that is not part of a unified knowledge-building enterprise. The reasons for this may lie in weak doctoral training, insufficient or inadequate mentorship, and tenure and promotion committees that are more concerned with quantity of publications rather than quality of publications. The greatest and most immediate changes probably can be made in the latter area. Through a top-down effect, tenure and promotion committees have the best potential for influencing the other elements of the research socialization process.

Another aspect of the issue of practice-relevant research is the apparent persistence of the practice-research gap. Identified as a continuing problem by Videka-Sherman and Reid a decade ago and echoed in the 1996 special issue of *Social Work Research* on the practitioner researcher model, this gap was again a theme in the chapters in this volume. To the extent that this perceived gap does exist, it suggests that the practitioner-researcher model has not lived up to its promise of integrating practice and research.

Thus, it is clearly time to move beyond a narrow practitioner-researcher model to a broader conceptualization of research in practice. Fuller offers such a broader conceptualization in his notion of "reflexive practice." The reflexive, or research-minded, practitioner uses a variety of research techniques to continually monitor his or her practice and adapt it in response to the data obtained. Such practice typically does not entail the full application of the single-system design, but rather makes judicious use of particular elements of this and other methodologies.

There is some encouraging evidence that a substantial proportion of agency practitioners do engage in such broadly defined research activities. A survey of recent graduates of one U.S. school of social work (Marino, Green, & Young, 1998) found that over half of the respondents reported involvement in at least one of four types of research in their agencies, namely, single-system designs, surveys, qualitative methods, and quasi-experimental or experimental methods. These authors concluded that "If the ideal of the scientist-practitioner is expanded beyond engagement in single-system designs to include more empirical activities of practice, then our findings suggest the possibility that the model may in fact be thriving in agency-based social work practice" (p. 191).

The Practitioner Research Programme Fuller described provides one excellent example of how social work academicians may further facilitate agency-based research. U.S. schools of social work could consider establishing continuing education programs based on this Scottish model.

Alternatively, in view of Fuller's observation that the best of the projects carried out in the Practitioner Research Programme have been akin to a master's degree standard, perhaps U.S. schools of social work should consider reviving the master's thesis as a requirement for conferral of the MSW degree. Many schools dropped this requirement because it was too taxing on faculty resources. Perhaps if such theses were "shorn of the literature review and epistemological argumentation that sometimes disfigures dissertations," as noted by Fuller (p. 89), less demand would be placed on faculty time. A clear distinction could develop between master's theses and doctoral dissertations, with the former being more oriented toward practical agency problems, and the latter being more theory-based and intended to contribute to the general social work knowledge base.

We would recommend that these master's theses be carried out in the agency setting during the second year practicum. Several resources are available to assist students and educators in implementing such projects. For example, Westerfelt and Dietz (1997) provide a very clear, step-by-step guide for conducting agency-based research. We believe that requiring students to conduct practice-oriented master's theses would go a long way toward developing research-minded practitioners. At the same time, academic researchers also need to do their part to narrow the gap, by producing the types of practice-relevant research described above.

Another theme, addressed by Kahn, Kazi, and Fuller, is the epistemological debate. On this point we agree with Reid (1995) as cited by Kahn, that while "the controversy may have outlived its usefulness, it has encouraged careful methodological reassessments in social work research, has called for frameworks that favor 'diverse viewpoints', and given needed impetus to use of qualitative methods as appropriate" (Reid, 1995, p. 2045). Indeed, we would argue that research methods exist independently of any underlying epistemology. Thus, we advocate the methodological-pluralist approach described by Kazi and by Fuller. In this approach the choice of methods is guided by the research question, and multiple methods may be combined to yield a more comprehensive perspective on the research problem.

In regard to methodology itself, several authors (Kahn and Rosen, Proctor, & Staudt) remarked that many of the methods used in social work practice research are taken directly from the social sciences. Social work has few research methods of its own, and social workers have not substantially modified the methods of the social sciences. We would suggest that social work researchers should develop their own methods, or modify existing ones, to suit the profession's unique purposes.

Two areas would seem particularly suitable for such methodological invention and adaptation. The first is the area of intervention research. Rosen, Proctor, and Staudt described the purpose of social work research as being the production of control knowledge to inform interventions. In this respect social work research differs from the social sciences, and therefore this is a natural area for the development of social work-specific methodologies. Kazi's realist effectiveness cycle is one example of such innovation.

The second suitable area for methodological innovation is the person-in-environment paradigm. Although social work has long promoted this model as its basis for *practice*, few *research* methodologies have been based in this model. Most research methods pertain to either the person or the environment, but not to the interface between the two. Innovation is needed in this area in regard to data collection and analysis.

A final theme that arose in the preceding chapters is the issue of national organizational support for social work research. This theme was addressed by Kahn and by Austin, who provided specific recommendations for action by the National Association of Social Workers (NASW), the Council on Social Work Education (CSWE), and the Society for Social Work and Research (SSWR). Such actions include highlighting research-based presentations at annual conferences; developing a sustained funding base for social work research; and establishing staff positions within these organizations to support research. We concur with these recommendations.

In conclusion, we have abstracted several general themes for new directions in social work practice research that have recurred throughout the chapters in this book. A summary action agenda for the future of social work practice research covers two major areas: (1) conceptual and method-ological directions and (2) organizational directions. The following action items are relevant to each area.

Conceptual and methodological directions:

- Social work research needs to generate more knowledge about what interventions work, for whom, and under what conditions.
- The field needs increased application of developmental research models.
- Career researchers need to pursue systematic research agendas that result in cumulative knowledge-building, leading to the development and test-ing of interventions.
- The definition of the scientist-practitioner should be broadened to in-clude a variety of agency-based research activities.
- Methodological pluralism should be the accepted norm in social work research.
- Social work researchers should develop new and modified methodologies that differ from those used in the social sciences and that are suited to the unique aims of social work research.

Organizational directions:

- Schools of social work should implement initiatives such as continuing education programs and master's theses to facilitate practitioners' engage-ment in agency-based research.
- CSWE and NASW should establish a priority for the presentation of research-based, practice-relevant reports at annual conferences.
- SSWR should continue to sponsor national meetings for sharing research in all aspects of social work.
- NASW and CSWE, in cooperation with the Institute for the Advancement of Social Work Research, should develop a national strategy for develop-ing a sustained funding base for practice-relevant, replicable intervention research in a variety of substantive areas in social work.
- CSWE and NASW should establish fully funded staff positions to support the integration of research-based, practice-relevant knowledge into the educational curriculum, and to support its application by practitioners in the field.
- SSWR should continue to promote advances in the knowledge base of the social work profession, including the development of new and modified research methodologies.

References

Marino, R., Green, R. G., & Young, E. (1998). Beyond the scientist-practitioner model's failure
    to thrive: Social workers' participation in agency-based research activities. *Social Work
    Research, 22,* 188–192.
Westerfelt, A., & Dietz, T. J. (1997). *Planning and conducting agency-based research: A workbook for
    social work students in field placements.* New York: Longman.

Index

Note: Material presented in figures and tables is indicated by italicized letters *f* and *t* following page numbers.

About the Editors

Miriam Potocky-Tripodi is Associate Professor and Acting Doctoral Program Coordinator, School of Social Work, Florida International University. She is founding co-editor of *The Journal of Social Work Research and Evaluation: An International Publication,* is on the editorial board of *Research for Social Work Practice,* and is a consulting editor for *Social Work.* She is currently the secretary-treasurer of the Society for Social Work and Research. Her major area of research interest is refugee resettlement, on which she has published numerous articles. She also has written about research methodology. Her last book was *Social Work Research with Minority and Oppressed Populations: Methodological Issues and Innovations* (with Antoinette Rodgers-Farmer), published by Haworth in 1998.

Tony Tripodi is Dean and Professor, College of Social Work, The Ohio State University, and External Reviewer, Department of Social Work, University of Hong Kong. He is founding co-editor of *The Journal of Social Work Research and Evaluation: An International Publication* and is on the editorial boards of *Evaluation and Program Planning* and *The Journal of Social Work Education.* He is a past president and current board member of the Society for Social Work and Research and has written extensively about social work research and evaluation. His last book was *A Primer on Single-Subject Design for Clinical Social Workers,* which was published by NASW in 1994.

About the Contributors

David M. Austin recently retired as the Bert Kruger Smith Centennial Professor, School of Social Work, University of Texas at Austin, where he also served as Acting Dean from 1991 to 1993. He was chair of the National Institute of Mental Health Task Force on Social Work Research. He is the recipient of numerous awards and honors, including the 1997 Significant Lifetime Achievement in Social Work Education Award from the Council on Social Work Education.

Roger Fuller is Senior Teaching Fellow, Department of Applied Social Science, University of Stirling, Scotland, and former Deputy Director of its Social Work Research Centre. He has worked as a researcher in a variety of settings, including an English local authority, London's National Children's Bureau, and several British universities. He has published widely in the field of social work research, with particular interests in the evaluative study of social work, social work with children and young people, and the promotion of practitioner research.

Alfred J. Kahn is Professor Emeritus, Special Research Scholar, and Special Lecturer, School of Social Work, Columbia University. He also is co-director of the Cross-National Studies Research Program at Columbia, and Distinguished Visiting Professor at the Fordham University School for Social Work. He is the author of over 30 books and more than 250 monographs, articles, and book chapters. His last book was *Family Change and Family Policies in Great Britain, Canada, New Zealand, and the United States*, published by Oxford University Press in 1997.

Mansoor A. F. Kazi is Senior Lecturer in Social Work and Applied Social Studies at the University of Huddersfield, England, and Director of its Centre for Evaluation Studies. His previous position was Service Manager of Rochdale Education Welfare Services and Team Leader for the local education authority's performance review team. He is currently involved in a number of evaluation projects in social work, health, and education settings in both public and voluntary sectors. His publications include *Single-Case Evaluation by Social Workers*, published by Averbury, and *The Working of Social Work* (with Juliet Cheetham), published by Jessica Kingsley.

Enola K. Proctor is the Frank J. Bruno Professor of Social Work Research, George Warren Brown School of Social Work, Washington University, St. Louis. She directs the Center for Mental Health Services Research and a PhD Training Program in Mental Health Services Research, both funded by the National Institute of Mental Health. Her research in health and mental health services has been supported by grants from the Agency for Health Care Policy and Research, the National Institute of Mental Health, the AARP Andrus Foundation, and the American Heart Association. Her work appears in social work, health, and mental health journals. She co-authored *Race, Gender, and Class: Guidelines for Practice with Individuals, Families, and Groups* with Larry Davis. She received the Washington University Distinguished Faculty Award in 1992, the National Association of Social Workers' Presidential Award for Excellence in 1994, and the Mental Health Professional of the Year Award from the St. Louis Alliance for the Mentally Ill in 1997.

Aaron Rosen is the Barbara A. Bailey Professor of Social Work at the George Warren Brown School of Social Work, Washington University, St. Louis, where he founded and chaired the interdisciplinary PhD program from 1967 to 1978. From 1982 to 1990, he served as the Zena Harman Professor of Social Work and as Director of the Paul Baerwald School of Social Work at the Hebrew University of Jerusalem, Israel. His current research includes development and evaluation of systematic planned practice as a clinical decision support system, practitioners' clinical judgment and decision making, and utilization of professional knowledge in practice.

Marlys M. Staudt is Assistant Professor at the College of Social Work, University of Tennessee. She holds a certificate from the Academy of Certified Social Workers. Her research interests are services to children and families and clinical decision making. The research on intense home-based services that she conducted for her dissertation was supported by the National Institute of Mental Health. She has published in *Social Work, The Journal of Behavioral Health Services and Research, Child and Adolescent Social Work,* and *Social Work in Education.*

RESEARCH TOOLS FOR SOCIAL WORKERS FROM NASW PRESS

New Directions for Social Work Practice Research, *edited by Miriam Potocky-Tripodi and Tony Tripodi.* This timely and provocative book helps you put your finger on the pulse of research in social work practice—past, present, and future. Contributors from the United States and the United Kingdom, all prominent social work researchers, offer a variety of critical assessments of practice research, provide a wealth of new data on the current status of research, and clearly lay down their own visions of the agenda for future studies.

ISBN: 0-87101-305-3. May 1999. Item #3053. NASW Members $23.15, Nonmembers $28.95.

Social Work Research Methods: Building Knowledge for Practice, *edited by Stuart A. Kirk.* In this unique supplementary text, students will learn different approaches to conducting social work research in their required research courses. Filled with recent examples taken from NASW Press and other research journals, *Social Work Research Methods* illustrates the latest approaches for diverse fields of practice, populations, levels of intervention, and methodologies. Designed to supplement all of the current major social work research textbooks, *Social Work Research Methods* is a valuable teaching aid for all levels of research courses.

ISBN: 0-87101-300-2. December 1998. Item #3002a. NASW Members $33.55, Nonmembers $41.95.

Advances in Mental Health Research: Implications for Practice, *edited by Janet B. W. Williams and Kathleen Ell, cofunded by the National Institute of Mental Health.* This book provides the latest scientific knowledge for treating the wide range of conditions and issues encountered in social work practice. Today, public policy deliberations and the health care reimbursement system are creating an urgent need to prove that social work mental health practice is based on scientific knowledge. *Advances in Mental Health Research* will help you work toward that goal.

ISBN: 0-87101-291-X. March 1998. Item #291X. NASW Members $22.35, Nonmembers $27.95.

Practitioner–Researcher Partnerships: Building Knowledge from, in, and for Practice, *edited by Peg McCartt Hess and Edward J. Mullen.* Practitioner–Researcher Partnerships meets the long-term demand for forging more successful and effective partnerships between the worlds of social work practice and social work research. This valuable resource explains how to deal successfully with differing outlooks on approaches and methods.

ISBN: 0-87101-252-9. 1995. Item #2529. NASW Members $25.55, Nonmembers $31.95.

A Primer on Single-Subject Design for Clinical Social Workers, *by Tony Tripodi.* This practical guide demonstrates how to build the single-subject design model into your practice without disruption and then use it easily—to make key clinical decisions, monitor the effectiveness of treatment, promote client understanding, and demonstrate accountability in clinical practice.

ISBN: 0-87101-238-3. Reprinted May 1998. Item #2383. NASW Members $25.55, Nonmembers $31.95.

Social Work Research. This journal publishes exemplary research to advance the development of knowledge and inform social work practice. It includes analytic reviews of research, theoretical articles pertaining to social work research, evaluation studies, and diverse research studies that contribute to knowledge about social work issues.

ISSN: 1070-5309. Published quarterly: March, June, September, December. See reverse for pricing.

(Order form on reverse side)

ORDER FORM

Title	Item #	NASW Member Price	Non-member Price	Total
__ New Directions for SW Practice Research	3053	$23.15	$28.95	_____
__ Social Work Research Methods	3002a	$33.55	$41.95	_____
__ Advances in Mental Health Research	291X	$22.35	$27.95	_____
__ Practitioner–Researcher Partnerships	2529	$25.55	$31.95	_____
__ A Primer on Single-Subject Design	2383	$25.55	$31.95	_____
__ *Social Work Research* (Member)	7001	$40.00		
__ *Social Work Research* (Student Member)	7101	$28.00		
__ *Social Work Research* (Individual Nonmember)	7201		$63.00	_____
__ *Social Work Research* (Library/ Institution)	7301		$87.00	_____
			Subtotal	_____
		+ 10% postage and handling		_____
			Total	_____

❏ I've enclosed my check or money order for $ _____.

❏ Please charge my   ❏ NASW VISA*   ❏ Other VISA   ❏ MasterCard

_____   _____

Credit Card Number   Expiration Date

Signature _____

Use of this card generates funds in support of the social work profession.

Name_____

Address _____

City _____ State/Province _____

Country _____ZIP _____

Phone _____ E-mail _____

NASW Member # (if applicable) _____

(Please make checks payable to NASW Press. Prices are subject to change.)

NASW PRESS
P. O. Box 431
Annapolis JCT, MD 20701
USA

Credit card orders call
1-800-227-3590
(In the Metro Wash., DC, area, call 301-317-8688)
Or fax your order to 301-206-7989
Or order online at http://www.naswpress.org

NDBI99